YEAR OF THE DOG

Stephens Press

Las Vegas, Nevada

YEAR OF THE DOG

One Year, One Team, One Goal

Kurt Voigt

Editors: Jim Morriss, Dennis Byrd, Harry King
Copy Editors: Michael Doyle, Jami Carpenter
Art Director: Sue Campbell
Production Designer: Scott Harmon
Publishing Coordinator: Stacey Fott

Cataloging in Publication

Voigt, Kurt.
Year of the dog : one year, one team, one goal / Kurt Voigt.
192 p. : photos ; 23 cm.
Summary: Chronicles the once-in-a-lifetime high school football team from a
public high school in Springdale, Arkansas, led by quarterback Mitch Mustain
and coach Gus Malzahn.

ISBN: 1-932173-64-1
ISBN-13: 9-781-932173-64-2

1. Football—Arkansas. 2. School sports. 3. Football players. 4. High school
athletes. I. Title.

796. 332   dc-22   2007
2006932472

STEPHENS PRESS, LLC

Post Office Box 1600
Las Vegas, Nevada 89125-1600

www.stephenspress.com

Printed in Hong Kong

For Will and Taylor

I'll always be your biggest fan

Contents

Acknowledgments

THERE ARE SO MANY PEOPLE TO THANK FOR THE OPPORTUNITY TO WRITE THIS BOOK THAT I'M NOT SURE WHERE TO BEGIN.

My family — Shannon, Will and Taylor — my friends, and my employer, *The Morning News of Northwest Arkansas* (which allowed me the time to complete this) — all have my deepest and most sincere thanks and gratitude.

My publisher, Tom Stalbaumer, editor, Rusty Turner, and sports editor, Chip Souza, probably thought I had gone mad when I pitched the idea of this book to them in the spring of 2005, but they all were supportive throughout the process.

Also, to those who helped me along the way with any questions or favors (*Morning News* photographers Michael Zamora and Tom Ewart, reporter Denise Malan, Derek Burleson of Channels 40/29 in Northwest Arkansas, *Hooten's Arkansas Football* magazine and Leland Barclay, author of the *Almanac of Arkansas High School Football*) — I offer the same.

I'll add to that list Jim Morriss, my editor for this book and someone who knows Springdale and Northwest Arkansas as well as anyone. Without his ability to act as a calming sounding board during my sleep-deprived flurry to complete this project, I don't know if I could have kept my senses long enough to do so.

Most importantly, I want to say thank you to the coaches and players at Springdale High, who allowed me to become part of their unique story — from the volleyball courts in Hermosa Beach to the moments before their biggest game. The friendships formed while writing this mean more to me than they'll ever know.

— Kurt Voigt

Foreword

LITTLE DID I KNOW IN 2004 THAT A YEAR LATER I WOULD BE A PART OF SOMETHING SO SURREAL.

As an assistant athletic administrator in the Little Rock School District, my first encounter with members of the Springdale community came that fall at a football playoff game at Little Rock Central. I already knew Springdale football coach Gus Malzahn and one of his assistants, Kevin Johnson, because we were all part of the same master's program in college, so when the Bulldogs arrived at Quigley Stadium I stopped by for a quick visit.

Before long, the two-way radio I carried with me was going off. The crowd coming into the stadium was growing, the visitors' side quickly filling up.

"Scogin, we need more (one dollar bills) at the gates."

While delivering the change, a Springdale man approached me — upset at being told he could not take his pocket knife into the stadium. It belonged to his great-grandfather, he said, and while I explained to him that he could have his place back in line if he decided to take the knife back to his car, he was concerned about missing the kickoff.

He asked if I would mind keeping the knife until the end of the game. I agreed, and by the end of the night, my pockets were full. The people of Springdale trusted me, a complete stranger, with their family heirlooms — all for the love of their Bulldogs.

It was just a few months later I accepted a job in the very community whose people had made such an impact on me at that game. Malzahn, also the athletic director for the Springdale School District, hired me to become his assistant as well as the volleyball coach at Springdale High.

One of the jobs Malzahn gave to me during the 2005 football season as part of my assistant athletic administrator duties was monitoring the sidelines during football games. It sounded like a great job at the time (even if I think Malzahn does still owe me a trip to the spa over that one). What I didn't realize was that nearly every high-profile college football coach in the country would want to be on the sidelines along with other fans from across the nation — all in addition to our regulars. Between the transplanted fans, Malzahn and his assistants, and the media following the remarkable season, there were seemingly more people on our sidelines than at the Super Bowl.

Requests for tickets would start coming in to secretary Kathy Hardin on Monday of each week. Lines would start forming shortly thereafter outside of the field house, leaving poor Hardin little time to complete her work between selling tickets and monitoring the never-ending flow of footballs which fans wanted autographed by the team.

The Bulldogs were special. Everyone wanted to see them.

We would open the gates for a 7:30 p.m. kickoff at 4 p.m. each Friday — with lines already having formed. The people came with their dinner (even calling to have a pizza delivered), blankets, and books— whatever they needed to kill the time before kickoff.

Those who couldn't get in would line up five-deep outside the chain-link fence on the north side of Jarrell Williams Bulldog Stadium.

Then came the playoffs — with more record crowds continuing to flock to Springdale. Coaches and players from other communities began showing up as their teams dropped out of the playoffs, along with fans from near and far. Other athletic directors would call with questions about that night such as where to park. My answer was always to take the day off and bring a sack dinner, because that was the only way they would get into the game.

Then, the state championship game: We arrived early to War Memorial Stadium, where I looked forward to the opportunity to actually watch a game (the sideline duty was handled by the Arkansas Activities Association).

What I didn't realize would happen was just how many people would come to Little Rock to watch what they had heard and read about all season. They were there to see the Bulldogs, this once-in-a-lifetime team. So many made the trip that my cell phone soon filled up with messages from those backed up in traffic on their way to the stadium. They said the crowds were like an Arkansas Razorback game day, and they wondered if I could get them in a side gate.

Because of the lines, some turned away and listened to the game in their cars outside the stadium in the parking lot. Others, realizing that getting in before halftime was unlikely, turned around and went home. Mind you, these were people who had driven from other states to watch what they called "history in the making of the greatest high school team ever."

Throughout the season, every time I saw the team I would see Kurt Voigt. He seemed to have a special interest in the team and would ask about details for this book that no one else will ever be able to tell as well. In this dream we were all living, he was writing a book about an incredible community and its passion for a team whose journey captivated a state and a nation. This story touches every angle of the dream. It will lead you through a journey that by far is one of the best sports stories you will ever read. You will have the 50-yard-line seat, hear the cheers, see the great plays, be a part of this wonderful community — all without standing in line or having pizza delivered. Then again, maybe you should, because you will not be able to put this book down.

What this football team did for the community of Springdale, the state of Arkansas, and throughout the nation is what athletics is all about. I am sure you will agree after reading this book. You will be an extended member of our family and our great community. The dream that became reality will now live on in your heart and in the stories that will be passed on for generations.

— Annette Scogin
Athletic Director, Springdale School District

Introduction

I HAD NO IDEA WHEN I TOOK THE JOB AS PREPS EDITOR IN AUGUST 2004 THAT THIS WOULD EVER HAPPEN. I wasn't even penciled in to cover Springdale football. In fact, I had planned to cover Springdale's rival, Fayetteville, until another reporter left the newspaper a week before the season began.

To be perfectly honest, I had no intention of ever writing a high school football book, or any book for that matter. Sure, I had privately dabbled in some various types of writing over the years, but I never felt completely comfortable in my attempts to live up to my childhood favorite — fantasy author (and the inspiration behind my love of reading) Terry Brooks.

It wasn't long after that football season began, however, that the signs that this is what I was supposed to do became more and more clear. Someone once taught me in a metaphorical sense that if you follow the roadmap you'll always find your destination. It was a lesson I had no choice but to follow while watching what will likely go down as the greatest high school football team of my lifetime.

There were so many signs, and they all tied together in one form or another. First, there was my first meeting with Gus Malzahn nearly ten years earlier, when he was just beginning to form his dynasty at the tiny private school in Springdale, Shiloh Christian. His wide-open style of offense had made my job more fun than usual, even if it had presented some deadline issues on Friday nights.

Later, following my father's suicide — and my battle with depression that followed — I traveled with friends to Little Rock to watch Malzahn's first state championship appearance with Shiloh. One of my friends was actually covering the game for *The Morning News*, while I went for no other reason than I needed to get out of the house — and away from my personal demons — and I had a great deal of respect for Malzahn.

That day turned out to be the turning point in my life, for it was later that night following the game that I met my future wife and mother to my two children. It was the night I began to put my demons following my father's death to rest.

A few years later there was another spontaneous road trip to watch Shiloh and Malzahn, one only made possible when the team I was covering lost in the playoffs a week earlier. It was a trip to watch the little brother of a good friend play for Malzahn, and it turned out to be quite possibly the most incredible night that Malzahn and the others there would ever experience. It was the night of Shiloh's 70–64 win over tiny Junction City in south Arkansas, a night that began with the lights going dark shortly before kickoff and ending hours later with Malzahn telling his team, "That was the greatest game I've ever seen."

The next year I made a third unplanned road trip, a 30-minute drive to watch a Springdale playoff game in Central Arkansas. Again, it was a trip only made possible by a loss two weeks earlier by the team I was covering, and it was a trip I decided to make only because of a hunch that the career of longtime Springdale football coach and icon, Jarrell Williams, might be winding down. It turns out that night in Cabot was the last game he ever coached.

It was during the 2004 season I saw the potential for the Springdale football team in 2005, potential to be both a regional, statewide and possibly even a national story. At the time I told Malzahn in the spring of that year of my intentions to write this book I had no idea just how big that story would become.

The road took us from the big cities of Los Angeles and San Antonio to the windy roads of South Arkansas. What started as a nice little story about a dominating team in a football-driven city turned into a national soap opera.

In between, all the signs kept pointing toward this book.

I fully realize when many of you pick up this book, you will quickly check the table of contents and thumb through pages until you find the ones dealing with the recruitment of one Mitchell Mustain. Before you do, please understand that Mitch's recruitment wasn't the foundation for the idea of this book. It started as simply a story about a once-in-a-lifetime team during the final year before a second high school began play in a football-crazy part of Arkansas. No part of the meat market known as the recruiting game was intended to be a part of this when I began.

With that said, when you read what Mitch and his family went through during the process — and their thoughts on those involved — keep in mind a few things. First, at no point did either Mitch or his mother, Beck Campbell, have any reason to tell anything but the truth about what was happening around them, particularly during Springdale's season. That was when I asked Mitch to trust me with what was going on in his life, for the purposes of detailing the situation for this book.

Thankfully, both Mitch and his mother did trust me, something I value more than anything I'll ever accomplish in my career. That's why, as you read his story, I ask that before you judge what anyone said in the heat of the moment you consider two things.

First, put yourself in the shoes of Mitch Mustain, who went from a carefree 17-year-old eager to have fun with his friends to the most talked about person in Arkansas for nearly a year. His every move, from who he was dating to a fender-bender he was involved in, was discussed at water coolers, on Internet message boards and on statewide radio each day. It was like the existence of a fish in a tiny, clear tank, unable to hide from the peering eyes of people he had never met while trying to make the biggest decision of his young life.

Then combine what Mitch was going through with the pressure he was getting from those around him to play college football at Arkansas. He was a longtime fan of the Razorbacks and had committed to play for them. That said, in the fall of 2005, he and most fans were upset that the Razorbacks were coming off a losing season. And neither the fans nor Mustain were happy with coach Houston Nutt's style of play, which was more outdated than Mustain was accustomed to at Springdale High.

It was a combustible combination, one that led to some hard feelings both before this book and more afterward, I'm sure. However, regardless of the events detailed in this book, they should not define Mitch Mustain, who at publication is on scholarship at Arkansas and playing football for Nutt. His future is far too bright to come under further scrutiny for what was quite likely the most hectic period he'll face in his life, and my hope is that his story will help the next person like him out there when it comes time to make his decision.

I also hope those who read this and followed the saga while it unfolded fully understand the impact their actions had on Mustain and the rest of his much-heralded teammates. It's one thing to be a college football fan — excited about the annual infusion of new and talented players. It's another completely to try and influence where those players go.

Perhaps the next time a Mitch Mustain comes along, those who read this will let the process play out on its own rather than pushing their hopes and dreams on someone else.

I hope you enjoy meeting an incredibly gifted group of athletes and their coaches, as well as getting to know a city driven by its love for them.

CHAPTER ONE
House of Horrors

MITCH MUSTAIN'S INITIAL REACTION WAS TO REACH UP AND PULL HIS FACEMASK DOWN.

It had become almost instinct for the quarterback after being sacked or hit hard, a way to momentarily collect his thoughts when something had gone wrong on the field.

Only this time, Mustain knew something had gone terribly wrong.

He tried to lift his right arm off the worn turf at Quigley Stadium, only to be greeted by a sharp pain in his forearm. It was the kind of pain he had felt before, similar to when he broke his jaw after falling from that tractor just before his seventh birthday. The pain was so sudden he instinctively reached up from the ground with his good arm, probing the painful area.

His first thought was to stay on the ground. He rolled over to his back while teammate Mason Price stood over him, signaling to the sidelines for the trainers once he saw the bulge in Mustain's right arm.

In the next moment, Mustain decided not to wait for the trainers, instead rolling over, his elbow digging into the ground to keep his forearm off the grass. He then used his other arm to lift himself up and pull out his mouthpiece as he stood.

He had only taken a few short, wobbly steps toward the sideline before being met by team trainer Jamie Croley.

"It's broken," Mustain told Croley as they met.

Mustain could feel the bones shifting under his skin, and when Croley stopped the quarterback to feel his arm, the Springdale trainer knew Mustain's spontaneous diagnosis was a correct one.

As they started to walk toward the sideline, with Croley holding his arm, Mustain nearly collapsed. His head was fuzzy from the pain, and after a few steps he bent down with his left arm outstretched. He was seemingly headed back to the ground before his fingers grazed the grass below — a touch that caused his senses to snap back.

Mustain pulled himself back up, the haze replaced by anger at the thought of coming out of a game in which the Bulldogs were losing, 20–0. He felt the reason for the deficit was his fault, and in his next eight steps the magnitude of his failure set in.

Croley motioned to Springdale coach Gus Malzahn on the sideline that it was indeed the right arm that was injured. A few steps later Mustain looked down and caught a glimpse of his mouthpiece still in his left hand.

With his good arm, he tossed the mouthpiece toward the sideline, his head lowering again as he reached up to unsnap his helmet.

All that was left was to wait for the ride to the hospital, leaving his teammates behind to try and clean up his mess.

• • •

Bernie Cox's philosophy on coaching high school football offense in Arkansas was nothing like that of Gus Malzahn.

Cox's power running attack was well known throughout the state; it had led the Little Rock Central coach to six championships in 29 years. But if Cox was the gold standard of high school coaches in Arkansas, it had been hard to tell in recent years. Before the Tigers won the championship in the state's largest classification in 2003, Cox's last title had been in 1986.

One of the biggest criticisms of Cox was his style of offense. While teams across the state were developing more of an aesthetically pleasing game — the passing version — and winning with it more and more, Cox entered his fourth decade of coaching still using the same basic approach he had begun with: Control the game by holding on to the football as long as possible, i.e., run the ball.

As one fellow conference coach joked: "Give (Cox) a two-touchdown lead, and it's over. He'll never let you have the ball back."

For Springdale's Malzahn, time of possession was the absolute last concern of his entering a game, be it against Little Rock Central or any other team. Malzahn's philosophy, which was crafted as a twenty-something in eastern Arkansas and later refined while building a nationally recognized power at the tiny private school in Springdale, Shiloh Christian, was to make the game "as long as possible."

He did so by utilizing a quick-strike, no huddle approach, which allowed him to get a first look at other teams' defensive formations before sending in plays. It was an approach that had resulted in numerous state and national passing records being broken under his watch, as well as the highest-scoring game in the state's history — a 70–64 Shiloh Christian win in the fall of 1999 over tiny Junction City High School in south Arkansas. It was also an approach — one he compared to a "fast-break offense" in basketball — that had endeared Malzahn to fans across the state.

Since Malzahn's arrival at Springdale High in early 2001, his offenses hadn't quite reached the level of success that he had orchestrated at Shiloh. For one thing, he was facing tougher competition every week — moving from one of the state's lowest classifications to the highest — as well as battling the ghosts of Springdale's past, a past filled with tradition set by previous coach Jarrell Williams, a tradition of hard-hitting defense and winning.

The no huddle attack was still his calling card during his first three seasons with the Bulldogs, but the wins hadn't come close to piling up like they had during his 63–8–1 run at Shiloh, a run fueled by a 44-game unbeaten streak between 1998 and 2000. Sure, Springdale had reached the state championship game in his second season in 2002, finishing 12–2, but that was a team whose identity was cemented more in the run than the pass, a team without the Malzahn stamp fully imprinted on it.

Malzahn's third season with the Bulldogs in 2003 had ended with an 8–4 record, and it had ended at the hands of Cox's Tigers. It left the coach with a 27–10 mark in his short stint with Springdale. Acceptable? Yes. The dominating football power in the state that the Springdale alumni, administration and school board had thought they were getting when they hired the phenom coach away from Shiloh to be both the football coach and athletic director of the state's second-largest high school? No.

• • •

The Springdale team that made the three-hour trip to Little Rock on the Friday after Thanksgiving in 2004 was vastly different than the Bulldog team that had fallen to Central a year before.

Springdale began the season ranked No. 2 in the state, behind only Central, and whereas the Tigers returned most of the key players from their championship team a year before, the Bulldogs entered the season with a new and talented — albeit unproven — look.

Leading the way for Springdale's new optimism was its junior quarterback, Mustain. The 16-year-old had gone 20–0 as a starter the past two seasons, both in junior high and with the sophomore team, and his rocket right arm appeared to represent the unofficial changing of the guard in Springdale.

No longer were the Bulldogs to be defined by their past; this was Malzahn's team, a team with a quarterback and players groomed under his system and ready to play his game.

The Bulldogs had made headlines during the summer with their play in Hoover, Alabama. If the regional 7-on-7 summer leagues — passing-only leagues without linemen — that many teams across the country participated in were preparation for state championship teams, then the Southeast Select 7-on-7 Tournament at Hoover was preparation for teams with national championship aspirations. It was a tournament loaded with college prospects and coaches eager to prove themselves and their teams worthy of national recognition.

There, in July of '04, with Mustain earning the starting job for the upcoming season over senior Dylan Adams, Springdale won the 16-team event. The Bulldogs defeated national power Evangel Christian of Shreveport, Louisiana, not once but twice along the way, including in the championship game. It wasn't the win, however, that made the most news back home in Arkansas. It was the news Mustain received following the event that put both him and his talented teammates on the collective radar for football fans across the state.

Shortly after returning home from Alabama, Mustain was told by Malzahn that University of Arkansas football head coach Houston Nutt had called to offer the quarterback a full scholarship to play for the Razorbacks. To those who had seen Mustain play at Hoover, the offer wasn't all that surprising, but it nevertheless put a great deal of pressure on a quarterback who was still over a month away from starting his first varsity game.

The first game that season was a rematch of sorts. It was at Springdale against Evangel, which on the strength of eight Louisiana state championships since 1992 — including the mythical national championship bestowed upon the Eagles in 1999 by *USA Today* — entered the game ranked No. 7 nationally. The game was played on the Saturday afternoon following the first Friday night of the season, a change made to allow the contest to be televised across the Southwest on Fox Sports Net.

As good as the Eagles were in 2004 — they went on to win their ninth state championship under Dennis Dunn — September 3 of that season belonged to the Bulldogs. It also served as a coming-out party for Mustain, who led Springdale to a 38–14 win after heading into halftime 14–all. Mustain kept Evangel off balance, throwing over the defense and running when there was an opportunity. He threw for 266 yards and a pair of touchdowns and ran for 78, including opening the fourth quarter with a 67-yard sprint — the signature play of the game.

The Bulldogs spent the rest of the regular season and the first two rounds of the playoffs proving they were the team to challenge for Central's throne.

The numbers were staggering. Springdale rode the momentum of the opening win over Evangel to 11 straight wins following it, and the Bulldogs did so in style — led by the flawless play of Mustain and a junior class whose combined talent left opposing coaches in awe. Entering the game against the Tigers, the Bulldogs had outscored their opponents by an average score of 39–6, despite sitting the starters for much of the second half in most games.

"My gosh, (the University of) Arkansas would be doing good to have those guys," remarked one opposing coach before facing Springdale, only half-joking.

More than five hours before kickoff at Quigley, a group of Springdale parents had already gathered in a parking lot outside the stadium. They included Beck Campbell, Mustain's mother and biggest fan, a fan who had predicted the Evangel win the week before the game.

A capacity crowd was expected that night, including many from nearby War Memorial Stadium where Louisiana State University was making quick work of Arkansas. Outside Quigley, Campbell and the rest of the Springdale contingent were confident their Bulldogs would fare better.

A few hours later, Central won the opening coin flip and deferred to the second half. The decision by Cox was the same one he had made a thousand times over, putting his defense on the field to set the tone. That Springdale was averaging 39.3 points per game and had reached the margin required to invoke the 35-point Arkansas mercy rule in all but two games that season wouldn't change Cox's style.

It was a decision that didn't surprise Malzahn, who would have taken the ball if the Bulldogs had won the coin flip. He also wasn't surprised to look up in the stands and see over 12,000 people packed into the dark and damp 68-year-old stadium.

The weather forecast that day called for a line of storms moving through Little Rock either during the afternoon or evening hours. No rain had made its way to Quigley by the opening kickoff, but its precursor — a driving wind — had. The only thing consistent about the intermittent gusts, some of nearly 30 mph, was the direction from which they came. They entered the stadium from its open end on the south and rushed through and over the brick wall that hid the field from street level on the north.

Springdale opened the game moving directly into the teeth of that wind. The Bulldogs had scored on their opening possession in 11 of 12 games that season, but they went three-and-out against the Tigers and the wind.

Defensively, the Bulldogs, who had six shutouts coming into the game, held the Tigers to start the game. However, on their next possession, a Mustain pass sailed high into the wind and off the fingertips of receiver Andrew Norman. The tipped pass was intercepted by Central's Kevin Thornton and returned 30 yards to the Springdale 12-yard line. Three plays later, the Tigers went up 7–0 after a one-yard run by quarterback Clark Irwin.

The Bulldogs didn't fare any better on their second drive, and a 23-yard punt into the wind after a Mustain sack gave the Tigers the ball just 43 yards from a second touchdown.

Springdale had trailed by no more than seven at any point during the season until Irwin found Thornton on a scrambling fourth-down play for a 24-yard touchdown pass, putting the Tigers up 14–0 with 1:53 left in the first quarter.

The two-touchdown deficit was more of a concern to the fans in the bleachers than it was for the coaches and players on the sideline. The team had scored 17 or more in a quarter eight times during the first 12 games and, other than the scrambling touchdown pass, the defense had given up just 34 yards on 11 plays.

Of greater concern for Malzahn was Mustain. The quarterback had struggled against the wind, with several passes sailing high. He also appeared both hurried and flustered by the Central rush, the first time all season a defense had bothered him.

Mustain appeared to have calmed down as Springdale finally mounted a sustained drive early in the second quarter, entering Central territory for the first time. At the Tigers' 20, Malzahn called for Mustain to fake a short pass to Damian Williams in the flat before looking deep down the sideline for Norman.

Williams jumped and waved his arms, doing his best to sell the fake, but the Tigers' secondary wasn't biting. Stuart Franks saw Norman heading toward the end zone the entire way, stepping in front of him at the goal line and picking off the pass.

All-out effort by running back Matt Clinkscales prevented a touchdown, but the weary defense yielded its third touchdown of the game two plays later. Even with a missed extra point, the Bulldogs were staring down the barrel of a 20–0 deficit, and Malzahn sent word for Adams to start warming up.

• • •

Mustain kept going over the day and the season in his head. He had just arrived at Arkansas Children's Hospital a few blocks away from Quigley, knowing his season was finished.

He held out hope, however, that his teammates would be able to rebound.

When the doctors and nurses began tending to him, his thoughts turned. The momentary doubt about his football future was slipping away, but the pain was not. Despite his arm being heavily wrapped while the nurses moved him around for X-rays, he could still feel the bones shifting next to each other in his forearm at even the slightest movement.

Doctors put him on a morphine drip after a short time, but filling the void of the pain was guilt, and it was solely his to bear. He had just played the worst game of his life on his biggest stage and nothing he could do at this point would change that.

• • •

Amidst the feel and sounds of disappointment immediately following the last snap, the tears could also be seen flowing down the face of Springdale senior linebacker Zach Pruitt, whose promising final season had just ended. Both of his hands reached up, tugging his facemask and helmet down, his eyes clinched so tightly that he wasn't aware of the direction he was walking.

Everything that had to go wrong for the Bulldogs to lose had done so. The wind, the early turnovers and the gradual wearing down of their defense, which was without its two best run stoppers, had all led the way to Rob James' 32-yard field goal with 18 seconds left to clinch the 30–21 win for Central.

Behind Adams, the Bulldogs twice closed to within six points in the second half. In fact, when junior cornerback Russ Greenlee picked up a fumble with 4:29 remaining and sprinted 57 yards for a touchdown to close the gap to 27–21, it appeared Springdale had a chance.

However, the loss of 306-pound defensive tackle Kyle Janus a week earlier to a knee injury took its toll on the Springdale defense in the second half against Cox's power running game. In 2004, that attack was spearheaded by bruising running back Mickey Dean, who rushed for 138 of his 156 yards in the second half.

It was Dean who carried the load on the final drive to the Springdale 11. From there, rather than going for a first down on fourth, Cox elected to try to seal the game with James. The kick would have been good from more than 40 yards.

As one reporter quipped following the field goal, surmising the feelings of many who were left of the crowd, "The question is, 'When is (Malzahn) ever going to win a championship if he can't win one with this team?'"

Central would go on to win Cox's seventh title a week later in a 41–7 rout of West Memphis. For Springdale, a season full of excitement, hope and future promise was over.

After the crowd had filed out of Quigley, Malzahn stayed behind to do his weekly television interview, his normal gameday twitching gone and trademark short answers even more bland than usual. He really thought this had been the game — and the season — that would start a back-to-back championship run like no other Arkansas had ever seen, but early nerves in the game had gotten to him, just like Mustain. Cox's style had gotten to him and it had showed in uncharacteristically aggressive play calling early on.

As the interview neared its end, the wind that had been such a factor early in the game stopped.

Moments later, the rain started to fall.

• • •

Back at the hospital, the morphine drip Mustain had been given started to take effect, numbing the quarterback's physical pain but not his mental anguish. His next battle had nothing to do with anything on the field; rather, it was the more than three-hour surgery he was facing that night.

It was a surgery during which doctors would place two metal plates in his forearm to help the bones heal, and he had been told that it might be as long as six months before he could participate in contact sports again.

He pushed aside concerns about his future when he looked up from his bed to see a family friend on the far side of the room, someone who he knew had stayed at the game. The somber look on the friend's face told him the result.

After three years of winning, it was official; he had lost and didn't know how to cope.

Except to cry.

CHAPTER 2

Welcome to Springdale

TWO TYPES OF PEOPLE CHOOSE TO LIVE THE COURSE OF THEIR LIVES IN ARKANSAS.

There are those who are born in The Natural State, are reared here and either feel so comfortable with their surroundings or uncertain of what lies beyond that they choose to stay. They grow up with a certain complex about their state when it comes to dealing with outsiders, but it's a complex lined by a fierce sense of pride in themselves.

Think Texans without Texas to back them up.

There are also those who come from elsewhere. By choice or by force, they arrive having already been indoctrinated into the feelings that many natives deal with every time they tell someone from the outside where they are from. For many locals, telling someone from either the East Coast or West Coast that you're from "Arkansaw" is a painful moment that you hope passes quickly and quietly, almost without notice.

For move-ins, their first such moment comes when they drive to their parents' house to tell them they are leaving Chicago, Los Angeles — or most anywhere else, for that matter. Or when they walk into their office one morning, only to tell their boss and co-workers they are moving to a place that is more associated with paper mills and agriculture than white-collar industry. They will swear they hear echoes of laughter when they walk out the door for the final time.

Once they arrive, they quickly realize the state itself can be broken down into three areas: Central Arkansas, Northwest Arkansas and everywhere else.

Everywhere else is described by some as a "third-world country," the place those who did the making fun of were referring to as their co-workers left. It's the Delta, the rice fields, the cotton farms, all the things more associated with Tom Sawyer or Huck Finn than modern-day America. It's a place full of shrinking populations and struggling school districts, all trying to sell hope to a group used to anything but.

The central part is the spot most likely visited by outsiders, its tourism highlighted by the state's capitol in Little Rock and a newly created Bill Clinton Presidential Library and Museum in honor of the country's 42nd president, the former governor who hails from a place called Hope, just a few hours down I-30. It's also the historic site of the Little Rock Nine, the group of high school students who refused to stand down in the face of segregation in 1957. The incident at Little Rock Central High School brought the eyes of the country down on the state when President Dwight Eisenhower stepped in and made sure integration was put into effect.

Little Rock and its suburbs, which have grown substantially since the white-flight took hold after the Little Rock Nine, had been the most identifiable part of Arkansas to outsiders for years, primarily as the state's leader in commerce and industry.

In the latter part of the 20th century, however, a change began taking place in the state, a change that would affect both the pocketbooks and feelings of those within it. As long as Arkansas has existed in its current form, it has been dominated politically by the Democratic party. That is, everywhere except the far northwest corner, where locally Democrats still ruled, but the region's more conservative nature showed in its Republican voting patterns in presidential elections. The hills that jutted up out of the Delta seemingly served as a barrier to the rest of the state's ideology and political landscape.

To many in the flatlands of Arkansas in the past, the term "hillbilly" had its origins in the northern part of the state, a way to even further isolate their poor neighbors to the north while enjoying the fruits of their own expanding oil, farming and manufacturing economy.

Their feelings were largely based on fact during most of the 1900s, especially as Northwest Arkansas grew into an area whose economy was spurred on by chicken farms and trucking companies, neither of which had an easy time even finding access out of their home region. That all changed in the late 1990s, however, with the opening of I-540, a stretch of interstate linking I-40 to the gold mine waiting at the top of the mountain, a gold mine spurred on, of course, by the world's largest retailer, Wal-Mart.

Well before I-540 made its way through the mountains of Northwest Arkansas with one man-made marvel of a bridge after another, the onslaught had already begun. People started coming, mostly a mix of affluent whites seeking corporate riches and a surging Hispanic population eager to find financial independence. They all came chasing the same dream, the spot at the end of the rainbow where everyone has a job and a better life.

Wal-Mart, Tyson Foods, J.B. Hunt . . . businesses whose names reverberated across the corporate landscape and throughout the country. All grew up in Northwest Arkansas and all were fiercely loyal to their place of birth. As they grew so did the region, joining the ranks of one of the country's fastest-growing places, as well as one of the safest and friendliest — a modern-day paradise.

The growth in the state's former stepchild was thought to be well received, its burgeoning economy good for all of Arkansas. However, over a century of separation doesn't go away overnight, and as the growth skyrocketed in the northwest, pockets of jealousy quietly rose up.

Subtle complaints could be heard at gas stations across the plains, outside the paper mills and through the pine forests. "Northwest Arkansas gets everything they want," they'd say. "Roads, schools, it doesn't matter . . . whatever. And what do we get?"

"Nothing."

Then, in the late 1990s, a flashpoint occurred. It wasn't something that made national headlines, but to those in a state where one thing and one thing only — the University of Arkansas Razorbacks — binds everything and everyone together, it was the biggest story of them all.

It was Frank Broyles, the longtime athletic director and former football coach of the Razorbacks, who suggested that upon the completion of a newly renovated football stadium in Fayetteville, home of the state's flagship university in Northwest Arkansas, perhaps all of the team's football games should be played there. It came in the face of years of history, years of a split home schedule for the Arkansas football team, a split between its true home in Fayetteville and its surroundings in Little Rock.

Again, to those on the outside looking in, and even some on the inside who had moved from the outside, the suggestion seemed a minor issue and perhaps even a no-brainer. Besides, why should a team continue to play three "home" games each year at War Memorial Stadium in Little Rock, they thought. Especially when, upon its completion, the Arkansas football team would have a palace with few equals right in its backyard.

The end result of the Great Stadium Debate between factions in central and northwest Arkansas was that the Razorbacks would keep at least two games at War Memorial Stadium into the next decade.

This illustrates the complex makeup of a state with just over a third of the population of New York City. The city might have its boroughs, and they might fight like family, but when the time comes to defend itself from an outsider, they join together — albeit with a little bit of brotherly nudging. The same can be said when the time comes to celebrate something grand, something unique and something so spectacular and out of the ordinary that its appearance is truly thought of as once-in-a-lifetime.

That's what the state of Arkansas had in 2005: something truly spectacular and unique. It came in the form of a high school football team from Springdale in the northwest part of the state.

Much like the rest of the state, the northwest also has its divisions. They are primarily broken down along what most refer to as the "Big Four," the four largest cities that line I-540 from south to north, nearly stretching to the Missouri border. Each of the four has its own identity or calling card, its own sense of individualism, though in order to sustain the rapid growth the boom has brought to the region, they are willingly forced to work together more times than not.

Their identities encompass young and old, and their accompanying stigmas stick with whoever lives in their borders.

To the south, Fayetteville is the college town, as well as the seat of Washington County. Its people are a mix of young and old, the students at the University of Arkansas and the legion of former students who never left.

The cities of Rogers and Bentonville lie only 20 minutes to the north of Fayetteville in Benton County, though their people couldn't be more different than their college neighbors to the south. Whereas Fayetteville relishes its reputation as the only bastion of liberal ideals and beliefs in a region known for anything but, its neighbors to the north equally relish their reputations as more family friendly and conservative places to live. If there is a buckle to the Bible Belt, Benton County might just be it.

Megachurches line the flat landscape of the county, which sits on a plateau between the mountains to the south and rolling hills of southern Missouri to the north. Nightlife in the two cities is an oxymoron, with alcohol only for sale at a limited number of restaurants throughout the dry county — just the way the people there have always wanted it.

Bentonville, with its picture-perfect downtown square, is a name recognizable to many outside of Arkansas, and it is still every bit the same place Sam Walton dreamed of when he started Wal-Mart years ago. A museum in his honor still sits on that square.

Today, Bentonville is no longer as sleepy as it was during Walton's beginnings, with Wal-Mart's headquarters the center of a global universe of commerce. Cars full of vendors all wanting to keep their items on the shelves of the world's largest retailer flood the town during the day, only to evacuate just as quickly to their homes at night. Since Walton's death in 1992, the company has made no secret of its desire to have its thousands of vendors within driving distance of its headquarters, and those vendors have heeded that desire, flocking to Northwest Arkansas from here and there, from everywhere.

Just to the east, the people of Rogers don't have corporate Wal-Mart to hang their hats on for an identity, but they do share much in common with Bentonville, evidenced by the fact that Wal-Mart No. 1 is still located in Rogers. Also, the two cities have grown so closely alongside each other over the years that it's nearly impossible to distinguish between their borders. In fact, along some parts of that border, some students from one city are forced to attend school in the other's school district, because the lines of education haven't kept up with the lines of rapid growth.

What Rogers does have more of than any other of the Big Four is easy access to I-540 on what previously had been undeveloped land. Most of the land now is developed or in the process. Upscale shopping centers, restaurants, and home-improvement megastores line the highway in Rogers, attracting many of the vendors who work in Bentonville and making the high school the largest in the state.

In the middle of it all, with an identity all its own, lies Springdale.

• • •

Much like how many Arkansans hold in an eternal sense of needing to prove themselves to outsiders, the same can be said of those from Springdale.

Originally named Shiloh after the church that occupied the site in the 1840s, Springdale was later renamed after an application was made to the post office and it was discovered that another Shiloh, Arkansas, already existed. It was a name derived from the many springs that supplied water to the area, though by any name Springdale closely retained its roots to the church.

Almost as closely identifiable with Springdale during its formative years was its agricultural roots, born out of the way its people made their livings. They did so by raising livestock on the flat lands to the south and west and in the meandering valleys to the east.

As Springdale grew through the early part of the 1900s, so, too, did its local industry. In 1935, Tyson Foods — now a household name — was founded. Before that, one of the region's largest trucking companies, Jones Truck Lines, came on the scene. Both helped form the foundation for the future of Springdale, the blue-collar neighbor to the north of Fayetteville and the University of Arkansas.

Today, the streets and stoplights are enough to frustrate even those who have lived in Springdale the longest. They've driven through the jumbled mess for the majority of their lives — watching the sprawl grow as Northwest Arkansas continued to boom. Much of their time on the roads is spent backed up in traffic on U.S. 71B, though sometimes they cut through neighborhoods in hope of finding a shortcut from one makeshift artery to another. Their purpose is all the same — shave as many precious minutes as possible in getting from one side of town to the other — for the roads simply have not kept up with the number of people.

Whereas Fayetteville and the hill country to the south abound with natural beauty — kept intact in part by strict building codes — the city of Springdale epitomizes urban sprawl as you head into town along Sunset Avenue. One fast-food restaurant after another greets you soon after exiting I-540, and one commercial building after another dots the path. There's no rhyme or reason to what goes where, just a never-ending maze.

At its core, along Emma Avenue, Springdale is anything but a scenic place to live. The street runs from west to east, cutting a path through the middle of Springdale High and crossing U.S. 71B on its way into the heart of downtown. Here, much of the history of Springdale still remains, even if it's only in the form of the brick buildings that once housed the history as it was made. The once-booming businesses, and the newest and most expensive homes, have fled downtown — leaving behind a shell of what Springdale used to be.

Ask the majority of college students in Fayetteville where they'd most like to live in Northwest Arkansas upon graduation and Springdale would likely be their last choice. They can't see themselves living in a place with the nickname "Chickendale," thanks to Tyson Foods and that awful smell that rises in parts of the city from time to time from its poultry processing plants and feed mill. What Fayetteville has in the way of culture with the college, Springdale has with the annual Rodeo of the Ozarks that takes place at Parsons Stadium the first four days of each July.

The funny thing is, once the same students do graduate from college their career paths likely will take them north into Benton County and Wal-Mart country — either for the parent company or one of the many vendors which supply it. They'll make their way through the same overmatched roads in Fayetteville for a while, trying their hardest just to get on I-540 before heading north. But soon after, the wear of the commute takes its toll. Their families begin to grow and time at home becomes more precious.

Eventually the time comes to move. When it does, many don't want to leave behind their college days altogether, nor do they want to venture too far away from the cultural heartbeat that Fayetteville provides for the region. Then it suddenly dawns on them — Springdale.

On any given day the booming heartbeat of Springdale thunders from across the city, circling the leftovers of what used to be. The sounds of new construction that can be heard throughout Northwest Arkansas are taking place here as well. New homes appear on a daily basis, from the planned development and cozy atmosphere of Har-Ber Meadows on the west side of town to more on the north and southeast sides of town.

Each year, the Springdale School District and its 182.3 square miles struggle to keep up with all the new faces — up more than 6,000 students since 1995 to an average of more than 15,500 in 2005.

It is growth driven by location and land as well as a surging Hispanic population — up to 35 percent of students in 2005 compared to five percent ten years earlier. Much like the families who move in to be closer to their jobs in Benton County, the Hispanics come to Northwest

Arkansas to take advantage of low unemployment. They come to Springdale because that's where their relatives have settled — and to put their children in a district that can claim annual test scores well above both state and national averages.

To cope, the school district is constantly looking for new land — new locations for future schools. Seemingly as quickly as the new homes sprout up across Springdale, new schools do the same, as the population closes in on 70,000.

The largest — and most expensive — of the new schools rose up on the west side of Springdale in 2005. It was the district's second high school, Har-Ber High, and was named after Jones Truck Lines founder, the late Harvey Jones and his wife, Bernice.

Many who drove up to Har-Ber for the first time mistook it for a small college campus, its massive white pillars marking the main entrance. The building was built to be a showcase of everything new and good in Springdale, from its energy efficient interior to its sprawling basketball arena.

The only drawback to Har-Ber's arrival in the fall of 2005 was the boundary line used by the district to determine which high school students went where. Instead of using a computer program to cut the city in half — with similar demographics for either school — the district instead used U.S. 71B as a "natural boundary," as one administrator called it. Those on the east side of the road stayed at Springdale High — except for a small area surrounding the high school, which sits just on the west side — while the rest were headed to Har-Ber.

In Springdale, where the majority of the new growth has taken place in recent years on the west side of town near I-540, west usually equals new and affluent. The east side of town, on the other hand, is often associated with poorer and Hispanic. The stereotypes turned out to be true with the new attendance zones, with Hispanics making up nearly 44 percent of the elementary students in the Springdale High zone. That compared to just 27 percent for Har-Ber. Also, a wide gap existed in the percentages of elementary students eligible for free and reduced lunches, one indicator of wealth.

Springdale High already had somewhat of a rivalry with the tiny private school in town, Shiloh Christian, but nothing that would approach what was likely about to happen. Springdale kids versus

Springdale kids. The "old school" Springdale High, with its worn look and rat-infested walls, versus its $35-million twin.

"The running joke is that it's going to be the football school versus the futbol school," one coach said.

• • •

Jarrell Williams answers the door and greets you with a handshake as firm as men 40 years his junior. The circles around his eyes are more pronounced than ever, the lines of time cutting through his tanned forehead.

As he begins to talk, immediately his voice causes you to listen more closely. It's not quite a shriek, but rather a gentle humming, a soprano without the song. It isn't a sound that to the untrained ear would be thought of as something that could instill fear, discipline or respect, but you know that's the case. It's a sound that begins deep in the back of his throat, but as the words come, you soon realize they are almost bouncing off the top of his mouth, seemingly sucking away any hint of bass before they hit the open air.

As he turns to lead you toward the kitchen at his home just a golf cart drive away from Springdale Country Club, you see the defined calf muscles in his legs, which still look like those of a one-time University of Arkansas football and baseball player. The strength behind his steps is still there, though he's currently frustrated at a back strain that has kept him off the golf course for several weeks.

If you had never met or heard of the man standing in front of you before, it wouldn't take you long to narrow down his former profession. You'd guess either military man or football coach from the way he carries himself as he walks, the way he looks you dead square in the eye — whether talking or listening.

This man was — or always will be, rather — a leader of men. And in Springdale, his legions number in the thousands.

He was more than just a football coach during his 35 years at Springdale High, a remarkable run during which he amassed a 262–132–4 record. It wasn't the 16 conference titles or four state championships, however, that defined Williams' stature in the city. It was his belief that playing the best brought out the best. It was his belief in the young men of Springdale. He was a mentor to the young men he coached, and later an icon to their sons. He helped give an identity to a city desperately seeking just that, and he did it through one thing — football.

Just a stone's throw to the north of Springdale High lies the testament to Williams' legacy. The field where he coached on Friday nights looks little today like it did during his time. It still has a quaint feel unlike many high school stadiums, thanks much in part to the lack of a track surrounding it. Fewer than ten feet stand between the edge of the turf and the first row of bleachers, separated only by a white picket fence that lines the field. The bleachers seat somewhere in the neighborhood of 6,500, depending on whom you ask. On many occasions throughout the years, however, more than 10,000 have found a place inside — and outside — the chain link fence to watch.

What they saw during Williams' tenure — more often than not — was a hard-nosed style of football. Sure, the coach would change his offense from time to time to keep up with the times, but more than anything the Bulldogs brought with them each and every Friday night something more important than anything he could coach — toughness.

Jarrell Williams made his way out of the Arkansas River Valley and through the hills that serve as the gateway into far Northwest Arkansas soon after graduating high school in 1957. He was born in a tiny town named Alma at the base of the Boston Mountains and spent his childhood moving back and forth between his birthplace and nearby Fort Smith, on the Oklahoma border.

Injuries and a lack of size derailed much of Williams' high school football career in Fort Smith. His sophomore year, weighing 137 pounds, a doctor told him, "something wasn't quite right" with the bones in his legs, a diagnosis that caused him to quit after the season. He sat out his entire junior year, only to return as a senior. Three games in, he broke his collarbone — ending his high school football career after just four games.

After the season, Williams received an invitation to play in an annual all-star football game, one he claims was meant for his twin brother Darrell, who started on the football team for three years. Afterward, he received a scholarship to the University of Arkansas for his performance, where he played for Razorbacks coach Frank Broyles.

Williams' first coaching experience came while playing American Legion baseball. That summer, he coached a group of Little Leaguers, later calling it "the greatest thing in the world." It was a memory he recalled after his first semester at Arkansas, when he made the decision to switch his major from business to education.

"Getting a coaching degree was the best move I ever made," he said.

He had been an assistant coach in Muskogee, Oklahoma, for one year when he received the phone call inquiring about his interest in a job as head football coach at Springdale. The call came from a Springdale school board member who had heard of Williams from a conversation with Broyles, now legendary for his ability to spot top coaching talent.

Williams' only tie to Springdale before the call was a high school game he had gone to while in college. That game was a matchup between Springdale and its most bitter rival, Fayetteville. Williams went to the game only because of his love for football, and while he can't remember who won, he does clearly remember the signs of a rivalry between the two communities. Other than that, the one thing he remembered most about Springdale as a college student in Fayetteville was, "Don't go up there because the police will arrest you," he said. He knew how important that part was even before taking the job, but during his tenure it became even more so. Fayetteville had the college, Benton County had Wal-Mart and Springdale had football — Jarrell Williams football.

He formed his teams around "good-ole Springdale kids," country strong and country tough. He built them from the ground up, requiring that the junior highs in Springdale run his same system to better serve as feeder pools of talent.

Under Williams, the Bulldogs never turned down bigger schools or better opponents. There was the state championship year of 1982, a year during which Springdale traveled to Missouri powerhouse Jefferson City and won — only to have things thrown at the buses on the way out of town. Later, there were tough losses to national powers such as Evangel Christian of Shreveport, Louisiana, and Jenks, Oklahoma.

"It took a while, but after a while we were able to compete with them and then it's a lot easier when you go back to playing in your own state and own league," Williams said.

After retiring following the 2000 football season, Williams settled in to the next phase of his life. His days were filled with golf and lunches with friends, where he'd often reflect on just what made football such an important part of life in Springdale.

"It's just the mindset of the people here," he said. "It's the parents, they have a great deal to do with it, and the administration, you know. It's just kind of a team-oriented deal for everybody."

Williams had also watched as Springdale continued to grow — bringing about the need for the second high school. He was more realistic than some about the need for the school. He knew better than most just how overcrowded Springdale High had become, and he remembered the countless faces he saw on the sidelines on Friday nights, many of whom were talented enough to play somewhere else.

"There's a lot of people sad about (the opening of Har-Ber)," Williams said. "A lot of people went to school (at Springdale High) and played on that field.

"It had to happen sooner or later. I guess we're a big city now."

Har-Ber High, its mascot name the Wildcats, opened in the fall of 2005. It did so as a member of the same athletic conference as Springdale High after the other conference schools voted to allow it to join in the middle of the usual two-year cycles used to determine size and classification. Har-Ber was eligible to compete in all varsity sports, except one: Football.

That would be reserved for one last run at a championship at Springdale High before the landscape would be forever changed.

It was the last year of the Bulldogs.

CHAPTER 3
A Spring Like No Other

THE MID-AFTERNOON SUN POURED OVER THE BLEACHERS ON THE WEST SIDE OF JARRELL WILLIAMS BULLDOG STADIUM, THE TWO-LEVEL PRESS BOX CREATING A FEW EXTRA YARDS OF SHADE NEAR THE MIDDLE OF THE ARTIFICIALLY SURFACED FIELD.

Gus Malzahn stood ten yards to the right of the shadow, his left arm pulled across his chest, his right elbow resting on the makeshift perch. Malzahn's right hand covered his mouth while the bill of his visor did the same for his eyes. To an untrained eye in the growing crowd in the bleachers, it might have appeared as if Malzahn were somewhere else on the warm May afternoon.

The truth was that he was deep in thought, but his attention was solely on the series of plays being run by the offense in front of him. He had noticed the more than 60 people, some of whom he didn't recognize, gathered in the home bleachers, but on this day he didn't have time for distractions.

Today was the opening day of spring practice for the Springdale football team, a series of five fully padded practices over two weeks in May. Today was the unofficial start of the 2005 season in Malzahn's mind, although the season's opening kickoff was still nearly four months away.

A pass by backup quarterback Jeremy Paxton, a junior-to-be, sailed high over a receiver and into the base of the white picket fence that lined the field. Immediately, Malzahn's head raised up and he put his arms down, quickly walking toward the offense. His foot had been tapping so quickly while the play was being run that several of the players not involved in the play noticed, but now that he saw a mistake he could correct, the tapping stopped. Instead of saying something about the pass to Paxton, Malzahn met the receiver as he walked back toward the huddle, quietly explaining to him that if he had done a better job of planting his feet into the turf, his break would have been quicker and the ball would have been catchable.

Here, Gus Malzahn was in total control. Here, all the distractions were gone; only football mattered. It was as close to calm as he had been in several months, finally able to put everything else out of his mind, everything but the game.

• • •

Kerry Winberry had seen just about everything high school football had to offer in his 33 years of coaching. He began in 1973 as a 24-year-old coaching eighth-grade football at Woodland Junior High in Fayetteville while still in college at Arkansas. Two years later, he was hired to coach the ninth-grade team at Central Junior High in Springdale, where he stayed for two seasons before joining the high school staff of Jarrell Williams as the offensive line coach in 1981.

In 1987, he was elevated to defensive coordinator under Williams, flourishing in his role as the quiet enforcer of a team that prided itself on fielding a tough, physical defense year-in and year-out. He had been part of two state championships with Williams, including Springdale's last in 1989, and that team set a school record, allowing only 8.4 points per game.

Winberry continued as defensive coordinator into the 2000 season. He and Williams thought that team that would end the Bulldogs' 11-year title drought.

What Winberry failed to pick up on during the season was what many of the players had guessed — that win or lose, this was going to be Williams' last year on the sidelines. To this day, Winberry can close his eyes and envision everything about Williams' last game and he still holds a grudge against his friend and former boss for not giving him a heads-up about his pending retirement.

There was a haze around the field that night in Cabot, forty minutes north of Little Rock. The lights shone down upon the players, glancing off the chilled air and creating an aura around them. The packed stadium was a bright jewel, set off by the pitch black outside.

Springdale was No. 1 in the state entering the game, although it had tied a game with intra-city rival Shiloh Christian, the tiny private school coached by up-and-comer Gus Malzahn. The Bulldogs had won their first two playoff games at home, and when Fort Smith Northside, led by future University of Arkansas quarterback Matt Jones, had lost at Cabot in the second round, Williams and Winberry felt like the main obstacle had fallen by the wayside.

What they weren't counting on was a series of bad snaps, several of which cost the Bulldogs possession and momentum. Making things worse, the backup center had quit the team just days earlier, upset at a lack of playing time and leaving Williams with no options.

The game went back and forth, yet the Bulldogs always assumed they would find a way to prevail over the undersized yet gritty Panthers. Springdale even had its shot to end the game on a short field goal with just seconds left in regulation, but a Cabot player found his way around the edge and blocked the kick, sending the contest to overtime.

It was in the extra time that the career of Jarrell Williams, the legend of Springdale and an icon throughout the state, came to an end.

"They ran the ball all night, and then they beat us on a dadgum pass," Winberry recalls of the bootleg to the left and eventual touchdown pass that won the game for Cabot, which went on the following week to win the championship. "It still hurts."

Afterward, when Winberry did find out about his friend's retirement, it was only natural that he would apply for the job. Many at the school expected him to become the new coach, given his experience and status as Williams' No. 2 in charge, and he was the one Williams endorsed, both privately and publicly, to take his place.

Everything changed on the last day the school district took applications. That was when Malzahn sent in his resume. It was a tactic he would later say was planned, both to keep his name fresh on the minds of those making the hire and to allow him to escape public questions over that weekend.

Whatever the timing, it soon became clear who the choice would be. Malzahn's name in Springdale was nearly as recognizable as that of Williams, thanks to his 63–8–1 record with the Saints and pass-oriented offenses as well as the tie Springdale and Shiloh had battled to in 2000.

For Winberry, the hiring in early 2001 required him to swallow a good deal of his pride. He had faced Malzahn's offense on the field and he knew from an opposing coach's perspective just how organized and innovative he was. But he thought it was his turn, his reward for those 22 years of loyal service under Williams, his chance to be the head of the Bulldogs.

That first season, Winberry continued as defensive coordinator under Malzahn, helping his new boss learn the Springdale players and the schemes and tendencies of its opponents. The following year, his concerns about how he would fit in with a new staff became even more heightened when Malzahn moved a former Shiloh assistant, Kevin Johnson, into the role of co-defensive coordinator with him. The title was still there as was the input, but in reality the final decision making was Johnson's, leaving Winberry in more of an "advisory" role.

Despite the additional hit on his pride, the next three years were good for Winberry. Not only was his stress level less without the responsibility for calling plays on Friday nights, but he had come to truly respect both Malzahn and the rest of his friends on the coaching staff. He knew he was in the final years of coaching and he was more appreciative than ever for his time on the sidelines. His attitude and quiet toughness also made Winberry appreciated by both his fellow coaches and players, past and present.

"Any person it would be tough on," Johnson said. "He was open to everything we wanted to do, and I see what he did as an example for all our players as how to be part of a team."

So, just a few months after Winberry's fourth season under Malzahn had come to a close, he was in a reflective mood while sitting at a Springdale baseball game one spring afternoon. He had seen the attention being thrown at several of the Bulldog players during the 2004 season, and as the team began to prepare for its spring drills the hype was more than anything he had ever witnessed.

The offseason had been anything but quiet around Springdale football. Even Mitch Mustain's rehabilitation from the broken arm he had suffered against Little Rock Central hadn't stopped the college scholarship offers from coming in. The wave started in early February, and he wasn't the only Springdale player getting a lot of attention. Massive offensive tackle Bartley Webb had offers from Texas and Notre Dame, while receivers Damian Williams and Andrew Norman were on the target list of others. Also, tight end Ben Cleveland, who had moved to Springdale from Kansas before his junior year, had started receiving attention despite missing time the season before with a broken collarbone.

The offers themselves weren't a shock to Winberry, for he knew better than most what an impressive group the Bulldogs had returning in 2005. What had left him speechless at times was the amount of attention being given to "The Springdale Five," as they were now being called, on local radio as well as recruiting Web sites and message boards.

Every time he'd turn on his radio, morning or night, he'd hear people who had never even seen Springdale play talking about how important it was that the core group stay home and play college football at Arkansas. As a longtime fan of the Razorbacks, one who had even worked on the chain gang — marking down and distance — at Arkansas home games, Winberry didn't disagree with the callers or posters. He just had a hard time believing they were so interested in the future of a group of high school kids who hadn't even finished their junior years yet.

Besides, they still had business to take care of at home. That meant winning the state championship that had eluded them the season before, as well as the one which had eluded him since 1989.

He just knew though that the attention wasn't going to go away anytime soon.

"I mean, they're rock stars," Winberry said. "I don't think any of us are ready for what's about to happen."

• • •

Beck Campbell was furious.

Of course, to those who knew her, that was just another way of saying she was on her soapbox for the day. She could have been upset at anything, ranging from education to politics, but there was rarely a day where Campbell didn't have something to say about something or somebody.

There were those around Springdale who found it easier to dismiss the petite, 40-year-old blonde rather than take her seriously. That's what they had done during an ill-fated mayoral campaign a few years earlier. Keep her happy, they'd say. Pacify her, no matter what it took. But, first and foremost, keep her on your side in case she ever got on that soapbox about something you had done.

Beck Campbell was used to the havoc she created from time to time, but she also was used to getting things done. She had never been good at sitting in the background while others orchestrated events around her.

That was why after her son, Mitch Mustain, had put together one of the more remarkable seasons a Springdale quarterback had ever had before breaking his arm as a junior, Campbell put all her efforts into his future. Those efforts included hours upon hours of sitting in front of the computer, watching all of the Bulldogs' offensive plays from Mitch's junior season. She then clipped out his highlights onto a tape, which she sent to over 200 colleges across the country, along with a description of her son and his talent.

She was ecstatic when Mitch had been offered a full-ride to play at Arkansas before he had even thrown a varsity pass. It was where she had gone to college, and it was the school Mitch had always lived within 20 minutes of while growing up. Everything about the college, its state-of-the-art facilities, its spot in the football powerhouse of the Southeastern Conference, and its location just down the road, made the Razorbacks the perfect fit.

For Campbell, there was one drawback and it was major. At Arkansas, her son would be playing for Houston Nutt. An innovative offensive coach upon his arrival in Fayetteville in 1998, Nutt had made more news made more news in recent years for his job flirtations elsewhere than for his passing attacks back home.

Like many others, Campbell had watched over the past four years as Nutt used the lightning-fast Matt Jones at quarterback, off and on. Soon to be a first-round draft pick of the Jacksonville Jaguars as a receiver, Jones hadn't been the prototypical dropback passer that Nutt could trust with his offense, but Jones' elusiveness and speed were too much to ignore.

The downside of using Jones as a run-first quarterback was the perception that was attached. Every time the Razorbacks trotted out in a power running formation or some other run/option-based attack, the notion that Nutt had gone conservative spread. In the homes of potential recruits, such a perception could discourage those who wanted to play in a wide-open offense.

One of those homes was that of Campbell and Mustain, who were eager to see what kind of response they would get from the highlight tape they sent out. The answer came quickly with offers from Texas A&M and Michigan State in early February. Others followed, seemingly

CHAPTER THREE: A Spring Like No Other   47

every day, with college football powerhouses such as Miami, Texas and Notre Dame joining the mix.

There had been some humorous moments during the flurry, such as a hand-written rejection letter from Wyoming, but as spring practice approached, more than 25 colleges had offered Mitch a scholarship. As the offers filed in, so, too, had the phone calls from reporters — from newspapers, magazines, television stations, and even Internet recruiting services.

Mitch had grown accustomed to dealing with the attention during his junior season, thanks in part to advice from Malzahn on how to answer questions without giving too much away. He knew to be polite and to smile. It was a breeze.

During the spring, Campbell's no-fear approach to dealing with people had served her well in dealing with some of the most well-known college coaches from across the country. She had no reservations about telling coaches the best way to recruit Mitch — with little pressure — nor about telling them to be wary of including Mitch's father, Gary, in the recruiting process. The two had divorced when Mitch was much younger, and Campbell had made it a point during one conversation to tell Nutt to ask Mitch whether or not he wanted Gary around during the process.

That's why she had been so furious as spring practice began, because sure enough, as she and Mitch had walked into a recruiting visit in Fayetteville just a few weeks back, there stood his dad and her ex-husband talking with Nutt, who she assumed had invited him without asking Campbell or Mitch first.

"I couldn't believe it," Campbell said. "I absolutely couldn't believe it."

On this particular day, as the second week of spring football practice continued in Springdale, Campbell's tirade was no longer about her surprise meeting during the recruiting visit. She forced herself to accept it was an honest mistake by Nutt and she had been too busy watching all of the college coaches — including seven from Arkansas on the first day of spring — file through the gates at Bulldog Stadium to watch practice. No, on this day her ire was directed at a pair of columns written by Dana Caldwell of *The Morning News of Northwest Arkansas* following a recent interview with Nutt.

The first, which had appeared over the weekend, was headlined: "Nutt Discusses Strategy For 'Springdale 5'" and the early part dealt with Nutt's feelings on the recruitment of the five talented Bulldogs, including Mustain. Because of NCAA rules, Nutt couldn't discuss the Springdale players by name or individually, but the columnist could, so he focused on them as a group, as well as the pressures of recruiting players so close to home in a state not used to such an occurrence.

"Today, right now today, I feel good," Nutt was quoted as saying in the column. "Two or three weeks ago, I didn't feel as good because you couldn't go over there. You hear about everyone else going over there, and you hear rumors of, 'He's going here. He's already committed.'

"And all those things drive you crazy. But you roll up your sleeves and say, 'Hey, we're going to protect what's ours, first and foremost.'"

It was the last part of the quote that infuriated Campbell, as well as a quote later in the column in which Nutt talked about those around the players pushing them to become Razorbacks. Just weeks earlier, Campbell had talked with Nutt privately about the upcoming recruitment of the Springdale players and how she and those closest to the players wanted to keep the local hype and external pressures as minimal as possible.

"He sat there and told me how sorry he felt for the kids and all the pressure they were under," she said. "And then he goes and does this?

"He basically just said that this state owns these kids, and it's their responsibility to go to Arkansas. Well, I've got news for him, nobody owns my son, least of all Houston Nutt."

The second column was headlined "Nutt and Malzahn could team up soon," and it started out with the statement that had Nutt known a few years earlier that Malzahn was interested in becoming a college coach, he might already be on the Arkansas coaching staff. Razorback quarterbacks coach Roy Wittke had been hired in early 2003, but Nutt inferred that he might have hired Malzahn instead, had he known.

"You know, when I found out that there was interest in him being a college coach, I was just on the day of hiring Roy Wittke — the day before, maybe one or two days," Nutt said in the column. "So, (Wittke's hiring) had already been in the process, you know.

"Forty-eight hours (earlier), I find out differently about (Malzahn's interest). I could've maybe already hired Gus Malzahn."

Campbell wasn't sure what to make of the second column, unsure if Nutt was reaching out to Malzahn, whose name was already being floated on message boards as a possible hire by the Razorbacks after the season. Or she wondered if he was trying to influence Mitch and the rest of the Springdale players by suggesting that they could possibly continue playing for their high school coach in college. What she did know was how the comments must have affected Wittke, both from a personal standpoint and in terms of job security.

"Do you realize what he just said there?" Campbell asked. "He just basically said that if he had known (Malzahn) was interested back then, he wouldn't have hired Wittke.

"Talk about not having any respect for your coaches."

• • •

As the two weeks of spring practice wore on, the influx of college coaches continued, as well as the discussions about the recruits on local radio and Internet message boards. One television station even cornered Notre Dame head coach Charlie Weis for a brief interview at the fieldhouse, putting it on air that evening.

Twenty-six colleges were represented by their coaches between late April and May during the flurry. A calendar kept on the desk of Malzahn's secretary, Kathy Hardin, was filled with the names of coaches and the colleges they represented. Only three of the tiny boxes on the May page were without the black ink Hardin used to write in the names and schools. It was a busy, busy month.

The schools were a venerable who's-who among college football powers across the country. In addition to Notre Dame, schools such as Oklahoma, Georgia, Tennessee, Texas and Miami were written down. Their coaches all made their way to Springdale to see what all the fuss was about.

One afternoon during the second week of practice, Kerry Winberry stood on the home sideline, watching the defensive linemen go through tackling drills. Of particular interest that day was the performance of Nathan Avey, No. 55. Avey looked the part of a football player in his shoulder pads and helmet, his 6-foot-2 frame and 231 pounds providing the ideal combination of speed and strength for his position.

The drill pitted a pair of defenders against three offensive linemen and a running back with the object to fight off the blockers and make the tackle behind the line of scrimmage. The first time Winberry signaled the play to begin, Avey blasted through the center-guard gap and caused heads to turn across the field when his hit on running back Adam Jones echoed off the stadium's metal bleachers. Just to see if the play had been a fluke, Winberry put Avey back in on the next play. This time, Avey put his right shoulder under the chest of a different running back, lifting him up and driving him backward into the ground.

"Wow, who is that?" one parent asked while sitting in the stands.

The reason for Avey's anonymity was also the reason Winberry and the other Springdale coaches were pushing him so hard during the spring. Avey had played football in Springdale in junior high and during his sophomore season, but before the 2004 season he decided to step away from the game, quitting the team. His reasoning to the coaches was that he had suffered a series of concussions — one major and three minor, he said — and that his family doctor had told him "it was probably time to take a break" from football. The logic was sound but anytime someone quit football in Springdale there were questions about their desire. In Avey's case, the coaches knew he had talent, but they quietly wondered if he was tough enough to handle a full season.

He had sat in the stands the year before for the win over Shreveport Evangel Christian, but he hadn't traveled to the season-ending loss to Little Rock Central. Watching his former teammates do well had been hard, but not nearly as tough as deciding to come back. Avey was approached at school first by offensive line coach Don Struebing, followed by Malzahn and Winberry before he started asking former teammates if they would have him back.

What they saw in Avey during the school year was someone who had spent much of his time away from football in the weight room with his older brother, a body builder. They also saw another body on the defensive line, where they had lost several players to graduation. The lifting minus the wear and tear of a season had added a good deal of muscle without any loss of speed or quickness. His former teammates saw the new look as well and they welcomed him back, the signal Avey had been waiting on.

He had been a contributor in junior high and as a sophomore, but nothing like what he had shown so far in the spring. Whether it was maturity or the newfound size, even Avey was surprised by his performance.

"Something just popped," he said. "When I came back all of a sudden I was getting off blocks easier and using my hands better."

For Winberry, the spring had been about more than just finding talented players such as Avey. He had enjoyed meeting the college coaches, but more than that, he enjoyed listening to what the outsiders had to say. One afternoon at practice, Winberry found himself standing next to Miami's Larry Coker, who had led the Hurricanes to a national championship in 2001 in his first season as a head coach after 22 years as a collegiate assistant. It was a career path much like Winberry had taken before being passed over for Malzahn.

It was Coker who turned to Winberry at one point and asked, "Do you realize what you've got here? You've got players out there you're probably not even thinking about that are going to be pretty good."

He was referring to Avey, though he wasn't the only one.

Another time Winberry was speaking with an assistant coach from Tennessee who said, "We go all over the country recruiting players. We go to all of these big high schools and we never see more than two that we would consider.

"You've got five, minimum."

The conversations only confirmed what Winberry and the other Springdale coaches already knew, but they felt good nevertheless.

Winberry, though, knew only winning a state championship wouldn't be good enough. There couldn't be one slip up, one loss. Heck, after all the attention the Bulldogs had received that spring, Winberry knew they couldn't even afford to look bad in a win to justify all the hype.

"People aren't going to expect us just to win," he said. "We've got to be perfect every week."

CHAPTER 4
Hollywood Bound

MITCH MUSTAIN CLIMBED ON TOP OF A STORAGE BIN NEAR THE END OF HOWARD JONES FIELD, THE FOOTBALL PRACTICE FACILITY ON THE CAMPUS OF THE UNIVERSITY OF SOUTHERN CALIFORNIA IN LOS ANGELES.

With his forehead beading up with sweat in the mid-afternoon July heat and his red, dry-fit tank top dampening up as well under the blazing sun, Mustain was thankful he had found a moment to sit down. That peace didn't last long. Soon after he had lifted up his blue sports drink to take a sip, another recruiting reporter — this one with a television camera on his shoulder — walked up to him and asked for "just a few minutes of his time."

Mustain didn't have the energy left to muster a smile, but he slowly nodded and reached his arms forward, pulling himself down off his temporary resting place. He walked toward the sideline, attaching a microphone to his shirt — something he'd become efficient at in recent months.

He had long since forgone normalcy in his life, ever since the scholarship offer from Arkansas the summer before. Whereas he once walked the halls of Springdale High in relative anonymity, his junior year had seen that change. Classmates he didn't know would walk up to him and congratulate him for either a Bulldogs win or his scholarship offer. It was a scene that carried over into public places at restaurants (with people asking for autographs) or while he was driving (others honking at him) — seemingly everywhere he went.

As Mustain talked with the reporter, he quickly discovered that he worked for one of the recruiting Web sites, looking for a video clip of the 17-year-old who had recently been named the top-ranked high school quarterback in the country. It was all about selling the future to subscribers, and what better way to sell than with future hope for college football fans everywhere?

This reporter, Mustain surmised, was from a national service based on the fact that all of his questions were about the recruiting process in general and not about a specific college. That made the interview easier since he wouldn't have to sugar-coat his answers to fit whichever school he was being asked about.

He listened intently to the questions, taking a moment to wipe the sweat out of his eyes. They were the same ones he had been asked thousands of times in recent months, so he had no shortage of practice in answering them. He had also seen all of the tricks different reporters used while asking the same question a hundred different ways — all wanting to know the same thing.

"So, Mitch, where are you headed?" the reporter finally asked.

It was a question Mitch wished he knew the answer to himself, one he thought he had answered at times over the past few months. However, standing more than 1,500 miles from home and under siege all morning from more cameras and tape recorders than he was used to in Arkansas, the answer was the same.

"Who knows?" he answered. "Who knows?"

• • •

Even as a child, Mitch Mustain's direction in life seemed almost predetermined. His mother, Beck Campbell, had wanted her second-born to be both a football and a baseball player from the day he was born on February 27, 1988, and much of his childhood was spent fulfilling that wish.

On his fifth birthday, Mustain's presents from his mother included both a baseball glove and football jersey. He was so proud of the jersey that he wore it at every opportunity, and he would become upset if it ever got dirty.

By the age of 7, the first opportunity for children in Springdale to play football, Mustain's fearless ways — born from his physical wrestling matches with younger brother, Matt — had already made him one of the more advanced players. He was the team captain for his first game that season. But what his mother remembered more was the embarrassment she felt that day when seeing her son walk on the field — with his Looney Tunes underwear showing right through his white pants.

As he continued through school and into junior high, Mitch's quick release and powerful right arm had set him apart from those around him. There was little doubt he was going to be the future quarterback of the

Bulldogs, a fact several of the high school coaches were already aware of. When he led the Southwest Junior High team to an undefeated record — followed by a perfect season as the sophomore team quarterback — predictions of greatness were already being made about his future.

"He had it all," Jarrell Williams said of seeing Mustain in junior high. "He could throw the ball better than any junior high kid I've ever seen, you know, and he was tall and could run.

"There was a lot of talent there, a lot of talent."

Growing up, his success in sports was not confined to football. From the earliest he could remember, his love for football had been equaled by only one thing — baseball. His right arm had made him a logical fit as a pitcher, and though the mechanics between throwing a baseball and football were different, Mitch's winning results were the same. While he only saw limited action on the varsity football team in late season games as a sophomore, Mitch was a key player that year for the Springdale baseball team — finishing 7–0 for a team that won the conference title.

Mitch's athletic success had been born out of an adventurous — and somewhat mischievous — nature as a child. If there was an opportunity to push the limits of his body, he always seemed willing to give it a go — even at the risk of bodily harm.

His first notable injury came at 15 months old, a third-degree burn on his right hand caused when Mitch — who had been outside while his dad, Gary, was working in the yard — reached up to touch the hot exhaust of a tiller his dad had just turned off. The burn ran from his finger tips to the bottom of the hand and resulted in a trip to the emergency room.

The next day, Mitch — showing little effect of the bandage on his hand — again found his way into trouble when he fell into a swimming pool. He was quickly pulled out of the water, but the fall meant the bandage — which was supposed to be kept dry — had to be taken off and rewrapped. When it was taken off, what Campbell and the doctor saw was that Mitch's whole hand had swollen up overnight; it was blistered and red.

"This can't be right," Campbell said.

The fall into the water proved to be a good thing for Mitch, the doctor told Campbell. If his hand had stayed wrapped underneath and kept dry like the emergency room physicians had prescribed, the doctor said there was a chance Mitch's hand would have been crippled with atrophy from the burn. Ten days of scrubbing off the dead skin until the hand bled prevented further problems, but the incident stuck with Campbell.

"It could have been all over before it ever began," she said of Mustain's athletic achievements.

Mitch's hand injury was just one of a series of childhood mishaps. There was his first birthday, when he knocked four front teeth loose after a metal chair he was standing on tipped over — resulting in a series of trips to the dentist. There were also the stitches he received in his ear after flipping over his bike and into a barbed-wire fence. And there was another trip to the ER for cuts around an eye after Matt body-slammed him into a trunk in their mother's bedroom.

"He was just a walking disaster," Campbell said.

By far, the worst of Mitch's childhood disasters came at age six. Campbell and Gary had divorced two years earlier, and one day Mitch and Matt were spending time with their dad on the family farm. The boys were playing in the bucket of a tractor their dad was working on when Mitch leaned out — suddenly becoming caught between the edge of the bucket and the wall of the barn. Gary's first instinct when feeling resistance from the bucket was to pop the clutch, something he kept himself from doing when he heard Matt yelling for help.

"It would have snapped (Mitch) in two," Campbell said. "Matt saved his life."

The injuries were severe. Mitch had been trapped, with the bucket running from his jaw down to his chest. It caused his teeth to separate from his gums, snapping his jaw in two places. Campbell was nearby at the time of the incident, driving oldest daughter, Sarah, and a friend to church when she saw Gary waving for help. As she walked up, she saw Mitch spitting up blood, barely able to breathe.

"I thought it had crushed his lung," she said.

The trip to the hospital left Mitch with his jaw wired shut for five weeks. Campbell was forced to put all of his food through a strainer, as well as buy several pair of pliers — just in case he became sick and the wires had to be quickly removed to avoid choking. Once the wires were removed, Campbell took Mitch to a local restaurant to eat whatever he wanted as a reward. Because his jaw was still sore from the wires and he was still unable to open his mouth fully, Mitch huddled over his spaghetti, slurping down a plate and a half.

So familiar with the happenings of the emergency room was Mustain that when younger brother Matt gashed his leg open in a bike fall at age six, Mitch was the one who explained what would happen at the hospital. Matt was so worried while waiting at the hospital that he wouldn't go see the doctor until he could "call bubby." Once on the phone, the two talked for several minutes, with Mitch calmly telling Matt that the doctors would clean the cut before stitching it up.

Mitch's broken arm as a junior in the loss to Little Rock Central was the second major injury that season for the family, following a knee injury Matt suffered in a junior high game.

As the arm injury healed during the winter and spring leading up to the summer before his senior year, Mitch's usual reckless nature had changed somewhat. He worried openly about whether he would play again, a normal reaction for an athlete during a lengthy and strenuous rehabilitation.

By the time summer arrived, however, Mitch was once again back to his usual self — carefree and relaxed with teammates and friends. He had gone through spring practice without any lingering effects of the injury, and after electing not to play baseball to focus on football, Mitch was ready to get back on the field.

In the meantime, there was plenty of fun to be had, racing four-wheelers despite protests from his mom.

• • •

Springdale's arrival in Los Angeles in the late hours of July 14 had been anticipated for months. In the spring, the Bulldogs were invited to the third annual Nike 7-on-7 Passing Championship on the USC campus. The invite came largely due to the presence of their quarterback and other top recruits.

The one-day tournament featured eight teams, seven from California and the lone outsider, Springdale. The event was less about competition – with just two guaranteed games and a third for the championship – and more about the recruits on parade. It was, however, a trip Gus Malzahn was excited about making. It was a chance to compete against top teams from elsewhere as well as a chance to promote both his players and school on the national scene.

Nike anted up $5,000 for Springdale for travel, but that wasn't nearly enough. Malzahn wanted to take both the 7-on-7 squad as well as the team's seniors — linemen included — as a reward for all their hard work.

"I don't care how we do it," he said. "I want to take them all."

So, Campbell went to work — raising money like many other Springdale parents had done before her on behalf of the football program. There was $10,000 from J.B. Hunt, $10,000 from a local car dealership and another $7,500 from Tyson. In total, she helped raise the $35,000 needed to take the 55 players as well as the coaches.

The money came with relative ease, much like it had for the video replay board and field turf at the stadium. Whatever it took, from paying for the weekly local television broadcast of Springdale's games to chartering buses for games such as the season opener in Shreveport, the booster club — on the shoulders of the work done by the parents — seemingly always found a way to get what Malzahn wanted.

With the event scheduled for the next day, the players and coaches flew out on July 14 from Tulsa, Oklahoma, two hours west of Springdale. Long delays, however, caused a large group of players not to arrive at their hotel next to LAX until well after 2 a.m. — just 10 hours before they were supposed to take the field. The next morning, the Bulldogs walked on to the field at USC in front of a curious group of onlookers. After learning where "the team in red" was from, one parent of a player on another team said aloud after Mustain had walked past, "A team from Arkansas flew out here for this?

"What are they, a college team?"

More than 50 friends and family members from Springdale also made the trip to watch the Bulldogs. Some flew out for a short getaway while others drove so they could stay for a while and reconnect with family, but they all came to see how their superteam would fare on such a big stage. They weren't the only ones curious, as several members of other teams could be overheard talking about Mustain and planning to watch Springdale play when they weren't in action.

"I think everyone out here is very curious to see this team they've heard so much about," said Greg Biggins, director of the event. "Really, I think Springdale is coming in here as the proven team, and the others are very interested to see how they match up."

In addition to the flight delays and short preparation time that morning, other issues were frustrating Malzahn. The team had brought its helmets — a standard piece of equipment in its usual 7-on-7 contests — but they weren't used at the event.

There were also different rules in the games, which were nearly twice as long as those back home. The biggest was that the games didn't necessarily end when the clock expired. If an offensive team had started a set of downs, it would be allowed to finish those downs. It was a minor difference, but one Malzahn wasn't used to dealing with and it came back to haunt him during the Bulldogs' first game against Valencia High. Springdale led 21–18 at halftime, but only after Valencia — led by University of Mississippi commitment Michael Herrick at quarterback — scored after time had expired.

Herrick stayed sharp in the second half and Valencia took a 38–27 lead with four minutes remaining. Mustain, however, rallied the Bulldogs — finding Andrew Norman with one of his six touchdown passes to pull within 38–33. Springdale then held Valenica on its next possession, setting up a last chance with under a minute remaining.

On the first play, Mustain and Norman connected on a 40-yard strike into the right corner of the end zone. Norman jumped over a defender to grab the pass that gave Springdale a 39–38 lead.

With time running out, Herrick completed two short passes to come within three yards of a first down at the 20. Instead of throwing into the end zone as time expired, he threw a short out to the sideline. The completion gave Valencia a first down and four untimed chances at the winning touchdown. Eric Jones nearly intercepted a Herrick pass on third down, but the Valencia right-hander found the end zone on the game's final play for a 44–39 win.

"We just scored too fast," said Springdale offensive line coach Don Struebing.

The Bulldogs went on to win their second game, 26–19, over Edison High, but they looked sluggish in the contest. The players were already exhausted from their long trip the day before, and the loss in the first game hadn't improved their collective mood.

Mustain impressed the crowd in his two games — finishing 32 of 59 passes with 10 touchdowns and just one interception. But away from the action, he was feeling more heat than just that of the blazing sun. Between games, a series of reporters — who had begun seeking him out in the morning — continued to ask for interviews and comments on his recruitment. Mustain was used to the questions, but he wasn't ready for all the attention heaped on him that day. He had hoped to concentrate on playing, and after the loss to start the day, he sought out a few minutes of solitude — only to have another reporter approach him. Finally, in order to escape the crush, he walked to the sidelines alongside Malzahn, who was watching another of the ongoing games.

After the win in their second game, many of the Springdale players — unsure of the event format — expected to play a third game in a loser's bracket of some kind. However, only the two teams that went 2–0 had a third game.

After learning that Springdale would not play a third game, Malzahn was thrown another curve by the Long Beach Poly coach, who approached him about playing an unscheduled game. The Poly coach told his players and organizers that he wanted to play Springdale, but his team went 0–2.

Malzahn was open to playing another game, but he was concerned about a lack of referees. All of the remaining officials were set to be used during the championship game, and he didn't want to play without some kind of authority keeping the game under control. His players were already upset about the earlier loss, and Poly was actively seeking out Springdale, so he knew things could easily get out of control on the field.

The two coaches met in the middle of a huddle of assistants to discuss the matter, with Malzahn finally saying that he wasn't going to play without officials. The Poly coaches turned and walked away, disappointed, just as the Springdale players were when they were told their day on the field was done.

"I don't want to play anything without officials," Malzahn said. "I know how it is. Our fans would get fired up, and I'd get fired up.

"We're not here to practice."

For his part, Mustain was somewhat relieved the day was over. He wanted to play another game, but he was also ready to get back to the hotel — away from the attention.

The next day, Saturday, was the day designated for fun. Malzahn had given the players two choices — either spending time at nearby Hermosa Beach or taking a trip to Universal Studios. The players chose the beach, but the coaches chose Universal. Malzahn volunteered to chaperone the players at the beach, spending time playing volleyball with the players against the backdrop of the Pacific Ocean.

While some wandered the beach, others rented bicycles and rode up and down the sandy stretch that kissed the ocean.

The day's activities came to an end well after dark when Malzahn and the players gathered to watch a championship boxing match between Arkansas native Jermain Taylor and Bernard Hopkins. Taylor won a close decision and the players cheered in the streets before returning to the hotel to prepare for their flights home.

The following Monday, less than 12 hours after returning from California, Malzahn sat in his office upstairs in the Springdale fieldhouse. Other coaches were at home, sleeping late following the four-day trip, but Malzahn was already back at work, anticipating the week ahead and looking back on the week that was.

He never said he was frustrated by Springdale's performance, but his body language betrayed him, hesitating before such phrases as "learning experience."

"Was it worth it from a competitive standpoint?" he asked while leaning forward in his chair. "No."

What bothered him more than anything about the trip was the way he had performed. All of that work and money spent on a chance to make a national impression, and he felt like it was his fault that the team hadn't done so.

The fact that the players had brought their helmets when they weren't needed; the uncertainty surrounding the rules of the event; even the format of the tournament itself, a format which led to Springdale playing just twice . . . All of the above, combined with the opening loss, gnawed at Malzahn for much of the trip home and still bothered him that morning in his office.

However, his attention was about to turn. This was "Hoover week," the final week of summer 7-on-7 preparation and competition which concluded with Springdale's return trip to Hoover, Alabama.

So, rather than continuing to stew about the negatives in California, Malzahn was busy trumpeting the positives, or one of the few he could muster.

"From a team-building standpoint, it was completely worth it," he said of the trip to Los Angeles. "The trip itself and the day everyone had together will help us down the road."

CHAPTER 5
Alabama Burning

THE BUS PULLED OUT OF THE PARKING LOT AT THE FIELDHOUSE ON WEDNESDAY, JULY 20, LESS THAN 72 HOURS AFTER THE BULLDOGS HAD RETURNED FROM CALIFORNIA.

Gus Malzahn wasn't on board; he had stayed behind that day to help serve as host of a quarterback challenge at Bulldog Stadium that culminated later that evening. The event was something he was closely involved with, serving as a teacher to all of the 15 quarterbacks from across Arkansas, and it was one that he felt helped promote high school football both in Springdale and the state.

Promotion of the state and Springdale was something he had hoped for a few days earlier in Los Angeles, but the constant hounding of quarterback Mitch Mustain by recruiting reporters had left Malzahn uncomfortable. He didn't blame the loss in California on the seemingly endless parade of media following Mustain's every move, but he was certain he wouldn't allow the same thing to happen again, especially not in Hoover.

The Southeastern Select 7-on-7 Tournament began in 2001 as a 16-team, invitation-only event, hosted by Hoover High School in the affluent suburb of Birmingham, Alabama. Entering the tournament's fifth year, the host school was coming off a third straight Alabama state championship, its fourth in five years under head coach Rush Propst. The school had finished 2004 a perfect 15–0, resulting in a final national ranking of No. 4 in *USA Today*. The only championship lacking from the resume of the Buccaneers was that of its own summer tournament against some of the best passing teams in the country.

Daphne, Alabama, had won the inaugural event, followed by national power Shreveport Evangel Christian, and Thomas Jefferson High School from Pennsylvania, the third year. As the interest grew each year, teams from as far away as New Jersey and California had contacted tournament organizers about possibly being invited to the showcase. It was one of many such events across the country each year, but its field, which boasted an average of 75 college prospects each year, made it one of the most competitive and most watched by the recruiting media. For those who attended the tournament, a complete media guide awaited, filled with details about each team as well as a list of its college prospects.

"It's kind of like the Super Bowl of 7-on-7," Malzahn said.

On Springdale's page in the booklet, that meant highlighting the 30 Division-I offers to Mustain, the 25 to Damian Williams and the 20 to Ben Cleveland. Andrew Norman also had five schools listed (Louisville, Michigan State, Arkansas, Kansas and Tulsa), while four other players — Russ Greenlee, Aaron Finch, Zack Pianalto and Matt Clinkscales — were also listed as college prospects.

In 2004, Springdale was invited to Hoover for the first time, largely based on the recommendation of Evangel head coach Dennis Dunn, who knew of Malzahn's offensive prowess from his days at Shiloh Christian as well as at Springdale High. The Eagles also were scheduled to play the Bulldogs in the season opener that year and the early peek at the other team was something both coaches anticipated.

Springdale made its mark quickly in its first appearance at the tournament, defeating Evangel twice, including in the championship game. The Bulldogs, much like Mustain, had entered the event as unknowns, but those days were long since over as they as they made their way back.

Following the quarterback challenge, Malzahn made the 574-mile drive from Springdale to Hoover straight through, arriving at the team's hotel at around 6 a.m. He did so on just a few hours of sleep, keeping himself awake by drinking coffee, singing '80s music and turning the air conditioner fan up whenever he needed a boost to keep his eyes open.

When he emerged from the elevator less than five hours later that morning, glancing over the collection of players gathered in the hotel lobby, his demeanor was far different than it had been six days earlier in California. His look was focused and his trademark twitching had returned. The constant adjusting of his watch, the tugging of his shirt, even the pulling of his pant legs, which his players liked to make so much fun of behind his back, were all signs it was gameday and that Malzahn was ready.

Whereas Los Angeles had been an unknown, Hoover was a place and a routine Malzahn knew. It was where he had won, and it was a tournament he had emphasized to his players for much of the summer. It was his opinion that the win here a year before had served as a springboard to the 12–0 start in 2004. He also knew that when the tournament ended, the Bulldogs had less than two weeks before the opening of two-a-day practices.

Another part of the comfort factor for Malzahn was the tournament's format. The 16 teams were divided into two, eight-team pools. Both of the pools would play all other teams over two days of pool play on Thursday and Friday, with seedings being determined for the double-elimination tournament from that. Unlike in Los Angeles, the games were 22 minutes each — just what Springdale was used to — with the clock running continuously for the first 20 minutes and according to normal rules for the final two. Points were given for touchdowns (six), interceptions (three), as well as a defensive hold (two) and an extra point after a touchdown if the offense could convert on one play from the five yard line. Two-point conversion attempts from the 10-yard line also were allowed after teams advanced out of pool play.

Also, helmets were required — unlike in Los Angeles — much to the liking of Malzahn.

"I really think this format shows who the best team is," he said.

The number of games — a team in the loser's bracket could potentially play as many as 13 over three days — was a tough task for any of the teams in the field. It was almost like a pre-August two-a-day boot camp to Malzahn, who relished the tough competition and opportunity to test his players.

Then there was the heat, which was nothing like the Springdale crowd had experienced before traveling to Hoover a year before.

"It's not like anything you've ever felt before," Beck Campbell warned before leaving for Hoover. "The air just doesn't move.

"Get ready."

• • •

If there was ever a polar opposite to the term "dry heat" often associated with the Southwestern part of the United States, its home was in Hoover, Alabama.

To simply say the kind of summer heat experienced by those who live in Hoover on a daily basis is a "wet" one wouldn't do it justice. The best example came on the Friday morning of the 2005 version of the Southeastern Select 7-on-7 Tournament. It didn't come from the players who were taking part in the event, but rather those who were watching the teams on the field.

Beck Campbell was wearing a white T-shirt and shorts when she stepped out of her car just after 8 a.m. The temperature wasn't yet uncomfortable and the sun hadn't started to bear down. However, after five minutes in the thick, humid air, sweat was beginning to drip from Campbell's forehead.

The opening evening of play the day before had gone as expected for the Bulldogs, who racked up three victories and outscored their opponents 97–34.

What quickly became clear on the second day of competition was that there were three teams with a legitimate chance at winning the tournament. Those were Springdale, the host Hoover Buccaneers, and Byrnes High of Duncan, South Carolina, the only team other than the Bulldogs to go undefeated in pool play. Byrnes was coming off of its third straight South Carolina state championship, had nearly as many college prospects as Springdale and had been the only team to defeat Hoover so far.

The only concern for Malzahn was keeping Mustain's concentration on the games at hand and avoiding a frenzy like had happened in California a week earlier. So far the problems had not been reporters asking where he was going, but rather fans in the stands doing the same — or at least trying to influence the answer to the question.

One man had arrived early enough that morning to park his car on the side of the road that ran directly behind the home stands. The Arkansas fight song blared from the car for more than an hour, the sound filtering down the hill above and throughout the stadium. One Bulldog player tried to put words to the music while walking from one field to another between games.

Hit that line! Hit that line! Keep on going,
Move that ball right down the field!
Give a cheer. Rah! Rah! Never fear. Rah! Rah!
Arkansas will never yield!
On your toes, Razorbacks, to the finish,
Carry on with all your might!

For it's A-A-A-R-K-A-N-S-A-S for Arkansas!
Fight! Fight! Fi-i-i-ght!

"Oh my God," Mustain said. "We can't get away from it anywhere."

There had also been the unidentified, twenty-something blonde female who had piqued the attention of the Springdale players while walking behind them on the track. When she passed Mustain, who had turned around to see what the commotion was all about, she looked straight at him and asked, without stopping, "Are you going to be a Razorback?"

"Who knows," he quickly replied, turning back around to finish his snack to a chorus of laughter from those around him.

Late in the day, between games, Mustain was approached by one of several recruiting reporters at the tournament. One reporter followed him as he walked from one field to the other, interviewing him along the way. From over 100 yards away, Malzahn saw what was taking place, and he made it a point to pull Mustain aside a few moments later, telling him to avoid talking to any other reporters until after the tournament. He had seen the distractions in California and he wasn't about to have a similar scenario play out at one of the team's most competitive events of the year.

"They're just going to have to wait," Malzahn said. "We're in the middle of something here. (Mustain) just needs to worry about the games."

Mustain had been frustrated by Malzahn's edict as he sat in the stands watching the action and waiting on Springdale's next game. On the one had he was relieved not to worry about dealing with all of the attention, but at the same time he wasn't very good at telling new acquaintances "no" when they asked for something.

"What's he expect me to do," Mustain said. "Just tell them to leave me alone?

"I can't do that."

Luckily for Mustain, his coach didn't mind doing that and he was put to the test after the Bulldogs' final game on Friday — a second-round tournament win. Springdale was still undefeated heading into the final day, but a winner's bracket semifinal against Hoover awaited at 8:30 that next morning.

After the game, Malzahn stayed momentarily on the field to talk with a few other coaches while the Springdale players made their way up the hill and to the team bus. That is, all of the players except for Mustain, who had been stopped by a local television reporter and his cameraman, seeking a few comments from the quarterback they had heard so much about. Mustain tried to explain to them that he couldn't talk, looking over toward Malzahn while he talked to them, but they insisted they'd take just a moment.

Malzahn turned from his conversation and saw what was happening. His voice rose from 20 yards away as he yelled, "Guys, this is going to have to wait until after the tournament." The reporter didn't say anything in response, his shoulders slumping as he pulled the microphone away from Mustain. Malzahn then turned and began quickly walking up the hill himself, ready to put the moment behind him.

"Can you believe those vultures?" he asked.

Miller Safrit, a recruiting analyst for Scout.com and one of the people in charge of nominating players for the U.S. Army All-American Bowl — a top high school All-Star game following the season — had watched Springdale for part of that day and said he understood Malzahn's position regarding the frenzy. He added that the attention is an expected part of the recruiting process.

"That's what happens when you have the consensus No. 1 quarterback in the country," Safrit said. "It's the sexy position."

• • •

During the first game on Friday morning, still while in pool play, Springdale struggled to earn a 23–20 win over Huguenot High School from Richmond, Virginia, a team that went on to earn the No. 10 seed in the tournament after pool play. The Bulldogs hadn't clicked on offense for the 8:30 a.m. start, and on defense they struggled to cover massive tight end Dedrick Epps, who had had offers from nearly as many schools as Mustain.

The next day, early morning problems again caught up with the Bulldogs. Three possessions into the game, the Buccaneers led 16–0. They had scored on a pair of touchdowns and a Mustain interception. Malzahn was clearly frustrated with the start, but he wasn't about to concede.

Instead, on Springdale's next possession, Malzahn told Mustain to look for his favorite play in the 7-on-7 format, a 40-yard strike down the right sideline to Norman. The two had run the play so often during the past two summers that the timing was second nature for both. Mustain would drop back and throw to a spot where he knew Norman would be, all within the four-second limit set for quarterbacks to release the ball.

The play worked perfectly, with Norman running past the cornerback and avoiding the safety, to get the Bulldogs back in the game, 16–7, following a five-yard extra point score from Mustain to Cleveland. After a series of defensive holds by both teams, Mustain again found Norman for another 40-yard strike, pulling Springdale to within 18–17 after a missed extra point try. He might have struggled at times during his junior season throwing shorter, touch passes — such as screens to running backs — but the deep ball had never been a problem for Mustain.

Hoover responded with a score of its own on the next possession and then held Springdale on its next, extending its lead to 26–17 with just a few minutes remaining. However, on a critical possession for the Buccaneers, Bulldogs senior linebacker Chase Davis knocked down a pass on third down to hold Hoover and pull Springdale to within 26–19 with 30 seconds remaining.

Mustain fired incomplete on first down, but on the next play he once again found Norman down the sideline from 40 yards out. Hoover still led 26–25 after the touchdown with 18 seconds left, and Malzahn called a timeout to think about his options.

He could attempt to tie and head to overtime with a one-point conversion from the five, or go for the win from the ten, which would put his team directly into the winner's bracket finals. He knew it would be tough to make the championship with two extra games in succession in the loser's bracket. A quick victory also would eliminate the potential for questionable calls in an overtime game against the host school.

"We're going for the win," he said.

The ball was placed on the left hashmark, with Norman out to the right. Mustain dropped back, looking to hit his best friend with a pass right over his left shoulder after he had cut inside the defender. But the pass sailed on him, too high for Norman to reach.

"Hey, we haven't played well early in the morning and we know it," Malzahn told the Bulldogs as they huddled up afterward. "Now let's get this one out of our system and come back to win this thing."

• • •

The stories of Gus Malzahn's ability to sense his surroundings are legendary among those who have played or coached for him.

When he was the coach at Shiloh Christian, Malzahn made it a point to constantly keep one eye on the stands and fence which surrounded Champions Stadium. His purpose was to keep anyone and everyone who might be associated with his opponent that week from watching — and possibly going home to tell the other team's coaches what Malzahn's players were doing at practice.

"He could spot someone if they were within a half mile of that stadium," one former player joked.

That keen eye was something Malzahn had brought with him when he became the coach at Springdale High. Whether they knew it or not, fans in the stands at every practice were identified by Malzahn as soon as they walked up the main ramp which led to the home stands and entered the stadium. The look might have lasted a split second (if you were from Springdale and he knew who you were), or it might have led to a huddle among the coaches (where he'd ask if anyone else knew who you were).

He'd also watch Center Avenue, where cars would stop from time to time underneath either the scoreboard or video highlight and replay board to its right. They'd park just outside the chain-link fence, lined with greenery on the inside, and watch through the open north end of Jarrell Williams Bulldog Stadium — with Malzahn watching them in return. Even though they were outside the stadium, that didn't stop the coach from occasionally sending an assistant to see who was inside the car.

"More than one of them have sped away," Malzahn insisted. "You just never know who's watching."

During the last regular season week of 2004, with Springdale undefeated, ranked No. 1 and favored to dominate a less physical and overmatched team from Rogers later in the week, a man on his late afternoon lunch break entered Bulldog Stadium and began to watch practice. Malzahn recognized the person as a businessman from Rogers, a respected member of the community — and also a resident of the city Springdale was preparing to play.

"I told him he was welcome to come any week to watch but that one," Malzahn said.

Springdale won that game 35–0, pulling its starters before halftime.

So it was of little surprise to those who knew Malzahn that as Springdale was preparing to take the field for the 7-on-7 championship against the host team that Malzahn's focus wasn't entirely on the game. During his pregame talk with Mustain, where he told the quarterback to use up more time with short throws and longer snap counts, Malzahn took a moment to look over his shoulder and into the home stands. He scanned the crowd, glancing from left to right.

"Where is he?" Malzahn asked.

After a few seconds, he raised his head to look at the press box high above, his eyes squinting through his wire glasses and under the heat of the scorching afternoon Alabama sun.

"Yep, there he is," Malzahn said, referring to Evangel Christian coach Dennis Dunn. The Eagles had lost more than three hours earlier, but Malzahn knew the coach would stick around and watch the Bulldogs in preparation for their regular season opener just over a month away. He knew Dunn would carefully analyze any formations Springdale ran that day, looking for anything new from when the two teams had played a year ago.

Anything to find an edge.

Springdale had installed several new formations and routes during the spring and summer, but once Malzahn saw Dunn he told Mustain not to use them against Hoover. He wanted to repeat but he didn't want to give anything away which might jeopardize the real season.

He also knew his team was physically exhausted after four straight games that morning — the Hoover loss and victories over South Carolina's Fairfield Central and Byrnes and Thomas Jefferson of Pennsylvania. In the first loser's bracket game, against Fairfield, it took a touchdown pass from Mustain to Norman with three seconds left to pull out a 22–17 victory.

Byrnes, the only other team to go undefeated during pool play, was next. It was a team featuring University of Georgia commitment Prince Miller at cornerback and highly recruited quarterback Will Korn at quarterback, and a team Springdale had lost to a year earlier. This time, though, Mustain threw for four touchdowns in a 30–21 win.

The Bulldogs started slowly in the loser's bracket final, falling behind Thomas Jefferson 10–0 after Mustain was intercepted. However, they tied the contest on a defensive stop by Russ Greenlee and pulled away,

26–13, on a pair of touchdown passes by Mustain, one each to Williams and Norman.

Hoover had played just twice that morning on its way to the final, with plenty of rest between games. If the weary Bulldogs could defeat Hoover, they'd have to turn around and try again since Hoover had no losses in the double-elimination tournament.

Malzahn knew the situation well, and that several of the team's starters would be unable to play in the final because of exhaustion. Linebacker Ryan Hoover sat on a cooler on the sideline before the game, hunched over with a wet towel draped across the back of his neck. Ben Cleveland lay on the grass just a few feet away, his legs beginning to tighten and cramp up. Even center Mason Price, whose only job during the day had been to snap the ball to Mustain, was feeling the effects, pouring water over his head and the back of his neck in an attempt to cool off.

The game hardly resembled the tight contest the two teams had played earlier in the day. At full strength, Hoover rushed out to a 19–0 lead over the Bulldogs on its way to a 34–15 win. Even Mustain struggled, his passes lacking their usual zip after so many throws over the past three days. Cleveland played, even scoring on an extra point catch, but most of his time on the sidelines was spent lying on the grass. As the game wore on Malzahn was forced to put his second team in, conceding defeat while also trying to protect his players from any more ill effects of the heat.

• • •

Ryan Hoover lay flat on his back on the shaded concrete underneath the home stands at Buccaneer Stadium, his arms motionless at his sides. Team trainer Jamie Croley rushed from the training room and back, gathering as many bags of ice as he could to put on the bare chest of the senior linebacker.

Just to Hoover's right, Ben Cleveland sat upright against one of the stadium support beams, his head slung back in pain as he held an ice pack against his thigh. He screamed loudly when a new bag was put on his other thigh, the pain of the cramping too much to keep in any longer. It had been just twenty minutes since Springdale's game had ended, yet the time had seemed like an eternity for these two Bulldogs who were battling the effects of all their action in the heat that day.

Cleveland had played sparingly in the final game and afterward he had started to leave the field with his teammates when he was stopped by a pair of reporters. In recent weeks Cleveland's stock among recruiting gurus had risen considerably, and the reporters confirmed that the tight end was headed on a series of recruiting visits across the Southeastern part of the country following the tournament. His face flushed and barely able to stand, Cleveland patiently answered their questions and had his picture taken.

Ryan Hoover had spent the final game on the sidelines, struggling just to keep his eyes focused. After the game, he and two teammates — Price and Cleveland — were taken to a hospital and treated with intravenous fluids and more ice. Though they fully recovered, the episode had put quite a scare into all involved.

The suffering players were the least of the concerns with many of the recruiting reporters after the tournament. The Malzahn-imposed blackout of Mustain had ended and he readied himself for the latest inquisition about his future by turning his hat around backward and tightening the ice wrap that was around his right shoulder.

"Here we go again," he said, turning to face the cameras waiting just a few feet away.

CHAPTER 6
No Calls, Please

BARTLEY WEBB NEVER FIT THE STEREOTYPE OF MANY OFFENSIVE LINEMEN. Sure, he looked the part — standing 6-foot-7 and weighing close to 300 pounds more than a month before the season was to begin — but he was far from the mindless, hulking oaf that some thought of when they saw someone his size.

His father, Perry, was the president of the Springdale Chamber of Commerce, and his lifestyle had always been one of means. That was particularly the case now at the family home near Har-Ber High on the west side of town, in the planned development of Har-Ber Meadows.

Perhaps Bartley was always going to be a thinker, a man more comfortable looking at his future than living in the moment.

One thing was certain as he readied himself for the start of his senior year —his teammates would listen to him first and foremost.

A man his size could have earned that respect in high school with threats or physical violence, but that was not Bartley. A funny story or a self-deprecating joke was just as effective, he thought.

"That's just not who I am," he said while standing on the sidelines in Los Angeles for the tournament there a few weeks earlier. He had traveled with the team as one of its seniors, though a lineman had no place on the field in 7-on-7 action. "People who don't know me look at me sometimes and think I'm probably not all that smart because of how big I am and I play football, but the truth is I just like to talk and get along with people."

Don Struebing was Bartley's coach on the offensive line for the Bulldogs, and it was through no part of his coaching that his star pupil had learned his friendly ways. Struebing had been a former high school All-American at Springdale under Jarrell Williams, and what his outgoing and sometimes bombastic personality had hidden off the field was a nasty demeanor on the field. Don Struebing loved playing the role of the tough offensive lineman, always bigger and meaner than the man across from him. It was that nature, along with a considerable amount of strength and skill, which had earned Struebing a scholarship to play in college for Arkansas, but a dislike for then head coach Danny Ford had led to a transfer to the University of Central Arkansas, where he became a Division-II All-American.

He hadn't been drafted into the National Football League after college, though he did get an invitation to a free-agent rookie camp. There were also Arena Football League offers out there for the taking, but with a wife and a nine-month old baby at home, his decision to stay in school and complete the final semester of his undergraduate degree had been an easy one. It was that decision which led Struebing onto the UCA coaching staff as a graduate assistant and later a full-time coach at the school.

"I could have been a journeyman, but I knew I'd never make enough to retire on," Struebing said. "So, I did the next best thing and became a coach."

In 2002, Struebing left UCA and returned to his high school alma mater to work under second-year coach Gus Malzahn. He was home, coaching on the same field where he had played.

Struebing's role grew in his four years .at Springdale, even though some co-workers still saw him as the man-child he had been in high school. He was the quick-witted jokester on the outside, but a worrier during game preparation. He often would sit alone during the coaches' meetings, agonizing over the diagrams of other teams' defensive fronts. In August, as practice began, there was no joking with players as he adeptly played out his role as the self-annointed tough guy on the staff. Despite that, his players loved and respected him.

What Struebing had seen in Bartley before his junior year was the same giant others did, but he also saw the gentle side of his new student. He knew the size would lead to opportunities for Bartley, and perhaps even opportunities for himself as the coach of a highly prized recruit. What he didn't know was whether or not the inner fire, the desire — the need — to completely humiliate and destroy opponents was there for Bartley. Struebing had that during his playing days, and no matter how much skill he had, the truth was that deep down he knew the reason he had been successful was that he was just plain tougher than the others.

During the summer leading up to Bartley's junior season, Struebing spent much of his time breaking down and humiliating the big lineman in front of his teammates. During practice, he'd ride him for incorrect form while backpedaling from his left tackle position, making him run the play over and over. He didn't let up even as Bartley headed for a water break, questioning his skill from afar. Bartley was one of five new offensive linemen on the team, but the way Struebing hounded him might have led some to believe he was the only newcomer on the line.

Of course, what Struebing was doing had very little to do with what Bartley would do on Friday nights for the Bulldogs. Truth was, even as a 271-pound junior, Webb's size and athleticism were good enough to dominate most defensive linemen he'd see. What Struebing was preparing Bartley for was his future in college football. Struebing knew well from his playing days that Bartley would have to work ten times harder to be successful.

"It's a whole 'nother world," Struebing said. "You've got linemen running like high school receivers, running backs flying like receivers . . . and every one of them are stronger than you believe."

After Bartley's junior season ended, college scholarship offers began coming in the form of letters, phone calls and text messages. With fall practice a week away, he had received 18 scholarship offers. He had it all, they said, the size, the skill and — as a bonus — he had the grades to be eligible right away.

There were so many opportunities that he didn't know where to begin. In February, during a visit to the University of Texas, both Bartley and Mitch Mustain thought they'd found a home with the Longhorns. They even talked of committing to Texas coach Mack Brown on the spot, but chose to go home and discuss the decision with Malzahn first.

That Monday after returning home, Webb met Malzahn at his office upstairs in the team's indoor practice facility. Malzahn had told each of The Springdale Five that he wanted them to make their college decisions before preseason practice began in August, his reasoning being that he didn't want the recruiting talk to overlap the season and become a distraction in any way.

So when Webb went to meet with Malzahn, he thought his coach would be pleased his decision was being made so early, even though he knew Arkansas fans would be anything but. Bartley Webb had grown up in Arkansas, and he knew as well as anyone the disdain Razorback football fans had for Texas, dating back to the days when the two schools played in the now defunct Southwest Conference before Arkansas had departed for the Southeastern Conference in the early '90s. He had heard all of the stories of classic games gone by and seen the rivalry renewed in both 2003 and '04 when the two schools had met — with each winning on the other's home field. He had also heard the people calling into the sports talk radio shows over the past few months and read the anonymous posters in the fan message boards for Arkansas, with the general consensus being that even if any of the Springdale Five didn't come to Arkansas, "they'd better not go to Texas," as one poster wrote.

He knew the history, but he also wasn't about to spend the next few years unhappy. He didn't like Arkansas offensive coach Mike Markuson, whom he viewed as arrogant for a coach coming off a losing season. He was also irritated that both Markuson and head coach Houston Nutt had virtually ignored him during the recruiting process. He also didn't think they really wanted him despite the scholarship offer. Most of all, he was uncertain about the future of Nutt, who he thought had worn out his welcome.

"He'll take the first decent offer he gets," Webb said of Nutt. "And then where will that leave me? Waiting to see who my new coach is?

"I don't think so."

Webb walked into Malzahn's office that Monday knowing his decision would cause some problems for his coach and his team, but certain that Malzahn would want what he wanted.

What happened next surprised, even stunned, Webb. As he told Malzahn he was thinking about committing to Texas, the coach became agitated in his chair behind the desk. His words were the right ones for the moment, congratulatory and supportive in nature, but Webb didn't hear them. He only noticed how uncomfortable Malzahn looked, shifting nervously in his chair and looking around the room constantly.

The meeting lasted only a few minutes, but it left Bartley unsettled and unsure of what his coach was really thinking. Bartley was so unhappy with the meeting, he told his dad of Malzahn's reaction. When Perry Webb talked with Malzahn the next day, the coach professed his innocence, saying he didn't realize he was acting in any such way and apologizing if he had. He would support Bartley's decision, no matter where he went, he said.

Just a few days later, Mustain left his house to make the short drive to Malzahn's house for a similar meeting. He was ready to commit to Texas, and it was time to tell his coach, though it was a different mindset that he professed upon his return home.

"All I know is that he left this house that day for (Malzahn's) house all ready to go to Texas," said Beck Campbell, Mustain's mother. "And then he came home talking about looking at all his options again.

"So, you tell me what happened over there."

As for Bartley, he eventually decided to drop Texas from the scenario, once the coaches there put a timetable on his commitment. It was a strategy used often by coaches of top colleges who wanted to shore up their recruiting classes early on, but it backfired in the case of Webb, who wanted no part of being pressured.

Once he really took time to think about it, his decision had been easy. He had grown up a Notre Dame fan and had felt at home during his visit to the campus in South Bend, Indiana. He also was enamored with first-year head coach Charlie Weis, who had been the offensive coordinator for three Super Bowls with the New England Patriots and was bringing his innovative schemes and straight-shooting style to the college game.

Bartley's decision became public while his teammates were in Hoover, Alabama, for the 7-on-7 tournament a week earlier. The backlash from those in Arkansas had been tempered somewhat by Notre Dame's national following, but it still had come, as expected.

One afternoon, Bartley was sitting in a chair in his living room when the phone rang. Before picking up, he reached across the table for a notepad, one that had a list of phone numbers scribbled on it. The phone number for the incoming call, which he glanced at on the Caller ID every time before picking up, didn't match any of the numbers on the list.

He answered the phone.

"Hello."

"What are you doing?" a voice on the other end calmly said.

"What?" Bartley replied.

"Just what in the hell do you think you're doing?" the man said back, the anger building in his voice.

Bartley hung up. He knew exactly what the man was talking about, and he was tired of dealing with others like him. Why people like him wasted so much of their time worrying about where he was going to college, he would never understand. It was his life even if he did decide to leave his home state for somewhere else, right?

Disgusted, Bartley picked up a pen next to the notepad. He looked back at the phone, copying the number on to his "Do Not Answer" list.

A few minutes later, the phone rang again.

CHAPTER 7
Summer of Springdale

EVERY COACHING STAFF IN THE COUNTRY HAS A DENNIS DEBUSK, AND IF IT DOESN'T, THEN IT SHOULD.

Officially, DeBusk's job on the Springdale staff was to coach the running backs. In reality, his position was that of designated team public relations director, team statistician, team traveling secretary, the one everyone else looked to organize the details of every trip or event.

His first year at Springdale, DeBusk was out of coaching, concentrating on his teaching duties. He had left Shiloh Christian, replaced by a young coach from Hughes named Gus Malzahn. In his second year, he joined Jarrell Williams and the other coaches he had come to know during 26 years in the business. When Williams retired and Malzahn was hired in 2001, DeBusk wasn't sure how he would fit in with a man whose philosophy was 180 degrees from that of Williams.

So he made himself invaluable. He took over the record-keeping duties, watching game film each week to determine official statistics as well as penciling in any records at the end of each season. He became the one who readied the official roster each year, designating numbers to new players. He was also the one who would call ahead on any trips, reserving hotel rooms and buses for the coaches and their families as well as the players. He was the one who solved problems before they were problems.

Sure, he still sat in on offensive meetings each weekend during the season, watching film with the other coaches. But in reality that time for him was a way to plan out his week ahead. Once he knew the basics of what the other team would do, he didn't sit in on the sessions between Malzahn, offensive coordinator Chris Wood and offensive line coach Don Struebing where that week's offensive plan was determined. Rather, he would take care of the small details for the week, such as drawing the numbers of the opposing team's starters and the formations they would run on both offense and defense on two pieces of posterboard, hanging them in front of the lockerroom for the Bulldogs to see and learn each day.

Of course, with eight assistant coaches — not counting a handful of volunteer assistants and trainers who helped during the week — Malzahn could spare DeBusk for the minutia. The 56-year-old's duties were as vital as game planning and appreciated by both the head coach and the players.

And then there were the stats, a normally mundane and often overlooked part of the weekend workload, but something that had received more attention during the past two seasons. After each game of the 2004 season, DeBusk was sought out by parents and media eager to get the official statistics. Three weeks from the beginning of the 2005 season, DeBusk was excited that Beck Campbell would distribute the stats. She ran the team's Web site, www.springdalebulldogfootball. com, and she planned to update the stats each Monday, reducing his workload and making it easier for those on the fringes of the program to keep up with their favorite recruits.

Another of DeBusk's duties was to help Malzahn any time an announcement needed to be made. Either Malzahn would have him make the phone calls to local newspapers and television stations, telling them a news conference had been scheduled, or he would give the list of numbers to Malzahn so he could make the calls.

DeBusk's help hadn't been needed when Webb's commitment to Notre Dame had been made public, nor had it a week later when word of Ben Cleveland's commitment to Florida had become public. However, when Damian Williams decided to join Cleveland in his commitment to the Gators and new head coach Urban Meyer, just a few days after August practice had begun, Malzahn had DeBusk make the calls, setting up a news conference after practice on August 4.

Malzahn elected not to allow Williams to talk to the handful of reporters who gathered that afternoon for two reasons. One, he wanted Williams to continue focusing on his work at practice that week, and second, he didn't want to rankle Arkansas fans any more than they already were — especially now that the first three of the Springdale Five who had committed to colleges (Webb, Cleveland and now Williams) had done so to schools other than Arkansas. Malzahn was worried that by allowing Williams to appear on television, the receiver would become the subject of even more criticism than he was already likely to undergo.

Williams' announcement was made in the form of a briefly worded, typed news release. It was handed out after practice that afternoon, and while Williams huddled with a few friends in the far corner of the indoor fieldhouse near the door to the lockerroom, Malzahn met with the reporters who had gathered.

Several players came out of the weight room just behind where the reporters were interviewing Malzahn. A player who had been watching the gathering provided some teammates with the first word of Williams' commitment.

"Wow, " one said, "That'll piss people off pretty good."

The manipulation of the media that afternoon wasn't the first time Malzahn had played such an active role in the method for delivery of information from one of his teams. He had become a favorite of many in the state during his tenure at Shiloh Christian, both for his winning ways and his desire to promote high school football in Arkansas and beyond.

More than once while at Shiloh, Malzahn had agreed to play games at neutral sites against larger schools for the crowds and the spotlight. In 2000, he took an active role in seeking out the intra-city matchup with Class AAAAA Springdale High, which came to fruition in front of an overflow crowd at Bulldog Stadium. That game also ended in a tie, leaving the Springdale fans and players wondering what might have been while the Shiloh faithful left full of confidence.

The next season when the two schools met, they did so at Razorback Stadium in Fayetteville. It was an opportunity, Malzahn thought, to bring in people other than just those in Springdale to watch a high school game, an opportunity to promote both the schools and athletes. Springdale, with Malzahn now at the helm, got its revenge that September night in front of an estimated 22,000 people. At the time, it was the largest crowd to ever witness a high school football game in Arkansas history.

"It's always about the kids," he said. "Whether it's the kids here today or the ones who are coming later on, it's always about them."

The ironic part of his promoting, which in turned helped his image as an innovator and future-thinking coach, was that Malzahn never did so by directly promoting himself. Almost as legendary as his high octane offenses was a bland public demeanor, one which he had carefully crafted over the years.

If you wanted to talk football, he'd talk football. If you wanted to talk politics, he'd talk football. If the conversation steered toward an uncomfortable subject related to something with his team off the field, he'd try and steer it back toward something on the field. If that failed and the subject was pursued, he'd fall back on one of his standard "I really know, but there's no way I'm telling you" answers. Reporter after reporter had tried to get to know Malzahn over the years by buddying up to him, only to be given exactly what the coach wanted . . . usually very little.

Rarely would Malzahn offer any insight into himself or what he was thinking away from football. And while part of that was Malzahn's desire to keep his life away from football private — his family and friends would talk about his outgoing personality and close relationships — the truth was that football was what drove Malzahn and anything other than that was an unnecessary distraction. It wasn't that he distrusted anyone new he met over the years, especially those in the media seeking stories on him and his programs, but rather it was their motives he questioned.

His promotional, yet tight-lipped nature had been put to the test like at no other time during the spring and summer. On the one hand, here Malzahn sat on the biggest sports story in the state, with fans of both high school and college eager for insight. On the other, he had to do everything possible to avoid dissension within his team, remembering tension that had built throughout the 2004 season when several upperclassmen became openly jealous of the attention heaped on the then juniors. Malzahn's main worry as two-a-days had begun in August wasn't whether Springdale was good enough to win the state championship. It was keeping the collective psyche of the Bulldogs focused on that task — and not on any outside distractions.

That is why as media attention intensified in early August, Malzahn began to take more and more control of just how much attention each player received. If a reporter asked for a picture of the Springdale Five together, then Malzahn insisted that the "only way" it would happen was if other key seniors from the team were included. Anything to avoid cliques and jealousy, especially as the battle for information regarding Mitch Mustain's college choice grew more intense.

Eventually, as it related to Mustain's decision, Malzahn decided the time for promotion was at an end. It was time to close ranks, with any information about Mitch's recruitment being kept between the quarterback, the mother and the coach. Malzahn had few concerns about Mitch letting information out too early. As for Campbell, however, he was never quite sure what she would say or how much.

That was why at one point, when a Little Rock TV station asked for an interview with Mitch Mustain's mother, Malzahn agreed to help, with a caveat. He wanted a list of questions so he could talk to Beck Campbell about keeping her answers short and to the point. The TV station refused, saying it wouldn't give the questions to the president of the United States.

"Well," Malzahn said. "Then you've about as good a chance of getting this interview as you do with the President."

During the spring, Campbell had made no secret of her desire for Mitch to go somewhere other than Arkansas. She didn't trust Houston Nutt, nor did she believe the coaching at Arkansas was good enough to prepare her son for the NFL. She knew there would be repercussions if Mitch joined Bartley, Ben and Damian in committing elsewhere, but she was far more concerned about her son than she was about unhappy fans.

However, her close involvement in everything from reminding Mitch to call coaches back to offering her opinion which schools he should consider, was causing problems between the two. He had always been an Arkansas fan, but growing up so close to the school, he was well aware of the many negatives espoused by his mother.

When it came to making a decision, Mitch's method was to relax and think about other things. The last thing he wanted to hear was what he should do or a recitation of the positives and negatives of each school he was considering. The conflict between the two finally came to a head late in the summer at the house of Andrew Norman, Mustain's best friend on the team and another athlete still pondering his college of choice. Campbell was upset at Mitch for not returning phone calls or taking care of chores and she went to Norman's home to tell him so. Once there, the two got into a shouting match with Mitch eventually walking out.

Soon after, word of the argument was posted on one of the message boards, leading to endless speculation by other posters about Campbell and her influence on Mitch. She had seen the untrue rumors of her sexual involvement with a Texas assistant coach posted on one board when Mitch was still considering the Longhorns, but this was even worse, she thought.

"They're out there putting every little detail of our life for everyone to see," she said. "Forget me, but how's (Mitch) supposed to deal with that crap?"

It was later that night that Campbell made a conscious decision to not bring anything further about recruiting to her son and she told Mitch of her decision. The pressure wasn't worth losing her son over, and besides, it was his decision, his life.

"I'm not telling him anything anymore (about recruiting)," Campbell said. "I'm done.

"He can do whatever he wants and I'll support him whatever he decides."

• • •

Andrew Norman didn't look the part.

Standing 6-foot-2 and weighing 180 pounds, no part of his physique caused the average onlooker to guess that Norman was one of the top high school football players in Arkansas, much less a member of the Springdale Five.

His stick-like legs made it appear he was always overmatched. No matter how much he ate or or much weight he lifted, Norman couldn't shake the label of the skinny kid who could catch a football.

As the recruiting buzz built, Norman grew used to second fiddle to his more heralded teammates. What he couldn't stand were those who doubted his ability, his determination to catch every ball. It was partly that doubt that caused Norman to play like a man possessed during 7-on-7 action. In both California and Alabama, Norman had led the Bulldogs in both catches and yards. He had done so with his usual effort, laying out for balls out of his reach and throwing his body around with little regard for his safety.

Take for example when the Bulldogs were in Alabama. There, during a loser's bracket game against Byrnes High of South Carolina, Norman lined up to begin the game against cornerback Prince Miller, one of the biggest recruiting prizes in the upcoming senior class. The 5-foot-10, 185-pound Miller, who would eventually commit to Southeastern Conference power Georgia, stood across from Norman, his chest and stomach muscles rippling through his blue, tight-fitting shirt. His bulging arms were defined down to the last muscle, the sweat glistening off them while the black visor he wore on the front of his silver helmet gave him the appearance of a warrior, an intimidator geared toward stopping the best an opponent could throw at him.

As for Norman, he unassumingly came to the line of scrimmage, looking back toward Mustain. He legs looked even skinnier than normal against the stout Miller and his helmet rode high on the back of his neck, giving the appearance it didn't quite fit. He knew who was across the line, but he wasn't about to let Miller know that he knew.

"That's a player right there," one recruiting reporter said of Miller. "Just look at him compared to (Norman)."

The snap came to Mustain, who dropped back. Norman, on the snap, could have faked left before cutting back to the right, but he didn't. He made no secret of where he was headed — he was going down the right sideline, straight for the end zone, and he wanted to see if his best was better than that of Miller.

Immediately, Norman ran past Miller, surprising the cornerback with his speed. Miller tried to make up the ground as Mustain let loose of the ball and he did so to an extent as the ball fell toward the ground just inside the end zone. His arms began flailing in an attempt to knock down what he couldn't see, even waving in front of Norman's face as they crossed the goal line.

None of it mattered to Norman, who had been watching the ball the whole way. The ball fell into his hands and he pulled it to his chest before tumbling to the ground with Miller on his back. He had beaten the best, skinny legs and all.

He would show them all, he thought — all those fans who were heaping all of the attention on Mitch, Damian and Ben. He'd show the coaches who thought he was too slight, too slow and of course, too white to play receiver in major college football. He'd show them all just what he could do.

Andrew Norman's father, Robert, had been an all-star receiver in central Arkansas during his high school days, and it became clear after Andrew started school that he shared some of his dad's athletic talent. The way he darted around the basepaths in baseball and his fluid work on the basketball court made Andrew a sure bet for success.

His dad also played a large role in Andrew's success, closely following his son's progress throughout the years. At baseball tournaments, Robert would be there. At basketball games, he'd be there. As Andrew made his way through junior high football and onto the varsity team in high school, Robert had always been there — watching both practices and games, talking with Andrew afterward about each performance.

Like many in Springdale, Andrew had gone through the youth football programs from the time he was in third grade. By the time he reached middle school, baseball and basketball had taken a priority over the gridiron, both because he enjoyed them more and he wasn't sure if he was big enough to play. He came back to the sport just before his eighth-grade year at Southwest Junior High at the urging of baseball teammate and friend Russ Greenlee. He began that season as a fourth-string receiver after missing several practices that summer while still with his traveling baseball team. After steadily moving up the depth chart, thanks to his quickness and sure hands, Norman eventually got his chance in a game after the starter broke his finger. He scored a touchdown in the game and became a starter for the rest of the season.

During his ninth-grade year at Southwest, Norman teamed up with Mustain to lead the Cougars to an undefeated season. A year later he had been one of a few select sophomores to play on the varsity squad. What made Norman successful on the field wasn't just his ability to snare footballs out of the air. It was his ability to catch them whether he was in open space or closely guarded.

He also had the benefit of deception against many opponents, a weapon that also was the cause of his greatest frustration. No matter how many cornerbacks he beat deep or how many passes he caught, he would always be labeled a slow, possession receiver because he wass white.

Norman had been happy for Mustain when his friend received that first offer from Arkansas before their junior years. After that season, however, he started to see just how college coaches across the country began to work when offers of his own started to come in. He also got an offer from Arkansas, where he knew his dad deep down wanted him to go, as well as offers from schools such as Louisville and Kansas. All of his offers were from some of the top conferences across the country, but they weren't on the level of offers to his other teammates. They weren't Texas, Miami, Florida or Notre Dame.

He had guessed the reason and he picked up on it during conversations with the coaches. For example, when Virginia had called asking Norman to fly out (at his own family's expense) for a workout, the coaches told him they couldn't believe he was 6-foot-2 based on the film they had seen. They also wanted him to run a timed 40-yard dash, and if all went well, they expected to offer him a scholarship on the spot. Norman wanted to make the visit, but he knew how expensive the trip would be. He had also picked up on the subtle implication made during the call.

Surely a white receiver can't be that fast, right? At least not fast enough to play major college football.

"I guess it's just a stigma about the white receiver. I mean, they didn't have to see Damian run, or Ben run," Norman said, referring to teammates Damian Williams (one of a handful of black players on the team) and Ben Cleveland (who played tight end). "I just said, 'I don't have to go out there and prove I can run. If you want to take a look at me, fine.'"

The more he thought about the calls and questions, the angrier he became. Just like Mitch, he had seen all of the talk about himself on message boards as well and he knew people doubted whether he was fast enough to play in college. He also knew those same people believed his scholarship offers had been part of package deals from colleges hoping to lure Mustain, since the two were best friends away from football.

"Let's be honest," one poster wrote. "Andrew Norman is a good high school receiver who is good enough to play lower division college football. The only reason he's getting these offers is because of the team he's on and his quarterback.

"Get one and you'll get the other."

Norman would shake his head when reading the posts. "Who do these people think they are," he said.

"That's all right," he continued. "They can say whatever they want, but I'll show them on the field and prove myself. That's what I'm going to do this year and it's what I'm going to do next year, wherever I am."

• • •

Mitch Mustain woke up just after 8 a.m. on Monday, August 15. He had known for all of that weekend of his decision to stay at home in Arkansas to play college football, but the decision hadn't yet been made public because he and Malzahn had decided earlier that he should wait — whichever school was the choice — for three days before telling anyone.

This was that day, and after his third night of sleeping on it, he was ready. He would announce after practice later that afternoon that he would become a Razorback and his life could return to normal. The hype and hoopla, the constant talk on radio, the rumor-filled posts on Internet message boards, were all about to stop.

After waking up, Mitch quickly readied himself and made the five-minute drive to the fieldhouse, where Malzahn was waiting. The two left a few minutes later to meet with Campbell one final time before Mustain would drive to the Arkansas campus to tell Nutt of his decision.

During the meeting, Campbell spoke freely about her son's decision and those who were influencing him during the process. She trusted Malzahn unconditionally, knew Mitch looked up to him as a father figure and that the two were nearly as close she and Mitch. Because of that, and the earlier confrontation and promise to herself to let Mitch make his own decision, Campbell didn't spend her time further questioning anything about Houston Nutt. Rather, she told her son, with Malzahn listening, to think hard about making the decision, think about the roles everyone was playing.

She wanted him to realize that no one, not even Malzahn, was completely objective about where Mitch was going to school. They all knew that Malzahn was likely headed to Arkansas after the season, a fact she reminded Mitch of as Malzahn listened.

As he made the 15-minute drive to the campus, Mitch was well aware of the pros and cons of the decision he was about to make. He had thought them through what felt like a million times over the past few months, and if he ever needed to see them written out all he had to do was read the message board posters who were doing it for him every day.

He recalled the distrust of Nutt by him and his mother, his doubts that Nutt would make good on a promise to change the offense, questions about Nutt's future, and his infatuation with other schools, namely Texas and Notre Dame.

In the end, he put those thoughts aside and focused on what he knew for sure. First and foremost, this was the college he had lived near his entire life. This was his school, and no amount of winning he could do in college elsewhere would trump the feeling if he could do it in his home state. He had seen the adoration heaped upon former Razorback Matt Jones during his four years at the school, the near cult following the sometimes bald, sometimes long-haired quarterback had developed.

He knew how badly Arkansas fans wanted a return to the winning ways of Nutt's early days at the school. Beyond that, they wanted a return to the consistent winning enjoyed while a member of the old Southwest Conference. He had seen the fans' elation when the Razorbacks traveled to Austin, Texas, in 2003 and defeated the Longhorns. He had seen the capacity crowd of more than 70,000 at Razorback Stadium in 2004 when Texas returned, defeating the home team late.

He knew the stories of great seasons and great games gone by. He knew all this about the fans because he was one of them.

Mustain also tried to believe Nutt's contention that the offense would change with the departure of Jones. Mustain also recalled Nutt's promise of more passing and Malzahn's rush to back the Arkansas coach on that point.

Another important part of the puzzle leading up to this day was what the continuing saga of his recruitment could do to his team.

After having lost in the semifinals the year before, and still with the thought that he was responsible for that loss bearing down on him, there was no way he was going to be responsible for anything that derailed this season.

The conversation with Nutt was a relaxed one, although the coach's over-the-top reaction caused a momentary thought back to just what a "dork" Mitch had thought his now future coach was at times during the recruiting process. He was used to Malzahn, who rarely even raised his voice at practice or before games, not even coming close to approaching the "rah-rah" style Nutt had employed during his tenure at Arkansas. Again, Mustain quickly put those thoughts out of his head, readying himself for another job he had to do that day before heading to practice and the news conference.

Besides, with his announcement done and over with, what did he have to worry about anymore? Now, he could sit back and help the Bulldogs win a state championship, all the while watching to see if Nutt really made all of the changes to the offense he had promised.

◆ ◆ ◆

Dennis DeBusk stood downstairs at the glass, double-door entrance to the Willard Walker Fieldhouse. Practice that Monday afternoon was taking place across the street at Bulldog Stadium, but Malzahn had excused DeBusk from being there.

Instead, Malzahn had asked DeBusk to stay at the fieldhouse that afternoon and help set up for a 5:30 p.m. news conference after practice. Malzahn had made the calls to local television stations and newspapers that afternoon, with his opening line being "It's happening today" before filling in the details of when and where.

Within minutes of when the phone calls began, word of the summons was already spreading on the message boards. On one, the subject headline read "IT'S HAPPENING," while on another "MUSTAIN PRESS CONFERENCE TONIGHT!!!!" screamed across the screen. At 1:30 p.m., when Malzahn began making his calls, 102 people were logged on to one popular board; within an hour of that, over 350 had made their way to the Web site after hearing of the impending news. All had opinions of what the news conference meant, although most agreed that if one was being held at all that meant Mustain was staying in Arkansas, just based on the fact that Malzahn had earlier kept a low profile when Williams had committed to Florida.

Back at the fieldhouse, DeBusk moved a table to the front of the film room where both Mustain and Norman would sit when they made their announcements. One media member asked what the decision was, but he said he didn't know the answer, and he was telling the truth. Malzahn hadn't told anyone, even his assistant coaches.

When practice ended just after 5 p.m., Malzahn walked out of Bulldog Stadium. As he turned the corner on the walkway on the south end of the stadium and looked toward the fieldhouse across the street, he couldn't believe what he saw. The parking lot, which had already been full of the players' vehicles, was now overcrowded with television news vans and a host of extra cars, all there to hear and deliver the news. One of the television trucks and its reporters had even made the three-hour drive from Little Rock to cover the event while casual fans had made the drive from across the area to attend.

Malzahn slowed as he looked at the trucks and the poles that rose above them, the instruments used to carry live satellite feeds across the state. He also saw the cables running through the doors and into the fieldhouse and the host of people filing in and out of the doors.

"It's going to be a circus in there, isn't it?" he asked rhetorically with a smile across his face.

It was as relaxed as he had looked in months.

• • •

Robert Norman wasn't smiling.

Actually, he wasn't moving at all, his entire body completely still and his face frozen with horror and amazement at what was happening before him to his son, Andrew.

Robert Norman had walked into the fieldhouse after practice that afternoon as proud as he could be of his son, who had told him earlier in the day that he was going to join Mitch at the news conference and commit to Arkansas. After meeting with Nutt that morning, Mitch had met with Andrew and sold him on the Razorbacks. Together, they visited Nutt and told him of the decision.

Robert had barely been able to control his emotions after finding out about the decision. Growing up a Razorback fan, he dreamed of catching touchdown passes for Arkansas while a receiver in the tiny central Arkansas town of Atkins, and now he was about to live his dream through his son.

Robert had been amazed when he walked into the fieldhouse to see seven television cameras lined up in front of the table set up in what usually served as the film room for players and coaches. All were there to carry the announcement live across the state, and they were joined by a horde of newspaper photographers and reporters who were seated in rows on either side of the table.

Ten minutes before the announcement was scheduled, Malzahn gathered his assistant coaches in the room that served as their offices adjoining the film room to tell them where both Mitch and Andrew were headed. The secret was out, much to the relief of several of the coaches who had privately worried about the reaction in the stands during the upcoming season if each of the Springdale Five had elected to leave the state.

Shortly thereafter, Dennis DeBusk, again serving in his public relations capacity, made his way into the film room. Once there, he stood at the front and laid down the ground rules for the gathered media that day. First, he said, Mitch would make his announcement, followed by Andrew. Afterward the two would be available for any questions for as long as was needed.

It was the reporter who broke DeBusk's rules who had Robert Norman paralyzed with fear and anger. All had gone according to plan during Mitch's announcement, with cheers in the room echoed across the state. However, as Mitch sat down, one eager reporter broke in, asking Mitch about his decision and Malzahn about the process. All the while, Andrew sat patiently, although inwardly he shared his father's feelings. When Malzahn regained control of the proceedings and moved on to Andrew's announcement, the same reporter continued with his live feed about Mustain while Norman was trying to talk at the front of the room.

The competing voices left Robert Norman and several other parents and spectators uncomfortable. When the reporter finally stopped talking, his station's live feed went off the air without a word about Norman.

Fortunately, Norman had become used to the hype surrounding Mitch, and the fact that they were best friends only helped diffuse what could have been a volatile situation. Of course, that didn't stop Mitch from unloading on the situation, because the entire time he was being asked questions about his commitment on live television he was thinking about this friend sitting next to him, waiting his turn.

"I felt bad for him," Mustain said. "It was like people just thought of him as an attachment."

"It annoyed me, and if it annoyed me, then I know it annoyed him, too."

After over an hour of questions and pictures following the initial announcement, most of those left at the fieldhouse made their way into the coaches' room, where they watched replays on the big-screen television.

DeBusk sat quietly at his desk, turning around in his chair to tell a group of parents behind him just what he thought of the entire day.

"I'm tickled to death," DeBusk said. "Now we can just play football."

CHAPTER 8
Fourteen Plays

THE GROUP OF THREE MEN STOOD ALONGSIDE THE CHAIN-LINK FENCE SURROUNDING THE FOOTBALL FIELD AT PRESCOTT HIGH SCHOOL, A 4½-HOUR BUS DRIVE FROM SPRINGDALE. Kickoff was still more than an hour away, but the men — all from the rural Southwest Arkansas town of slightly more than 4,000 people — had already stood along the fence that lined Cummins Field for more than 45 minutes.

They arrived an hour and a half earlier than normal, but not because of the 1975 class reunion taking place that night. They were there to see the group of football players they had heard and read so much about. Here, in an area of the state not often associated with statewide focus or attention, an entire community — one whose people pronounce their beloved town Preskit, not Prescott as it appears — was about to make its way to a high school football game to see the best show around.

Just six days earlier, Springdale started the season with a 35–7 victory over Evangel Christian in Shreveport. Evangel's only score came on the final play, a 2-yard run by Ramon Broadway, even though Malzahn had inserted his first-team defense in an effort to preserve a shutout.

Mitch Mustain had been less than efficient, completing 10 of 21 for 148 yards. He ran for a touchdown in the second quarter and threw a 5-yard touchdown pass to Ben Cleveland in the fourth.

One reason for Mustain's sub par day was that he was a bit off on several passes. Another was that the Eagles played their defensive backs deep for much of the game, inviting the Springdale running attack. It was an invitation even Gus Malzahn couldn't resist, despite a gameplan that stressed the pass. Another was that Malzahn had no desire to get his quarterback hurt in his first game back from the broken arm he had suffered 10 months earlier. He remembered the doubts Mustain had had about his future while rehabilitating his arm during the winter, and the talented defensive line of the Eagles had him concerned before the game. He was worried about what might happen if Evangel was able to pressure or sack Mustain — possibly shaking his confidence.

After Hurricane Katrina had ravaged the Gulf Coast, leaving much of New Orleans under water less than two weeks before, much was in flux around Shreveport in the days leading up to the game. In fact, with hotels filled with evacuees throughout the city, Malzahn elected to forego the reservations for Springdale and stay an hour north in Texarkana — allowing those displaced to be spared even further pain by being kicked out of their rooms for a football team. As for the game, Malzahn was in favor of playing despite the recent disaster. It was a feeling shared by most involved, although like many, Evangel head coach Dennis Dunn was busy housing displaced relatives the week before.

Five players affected by the storm had transferred to Evangel and all were immediately eligible to play under a ruling by the Louisiana High School Athletic Association. Malzahn was concerned about the unknown, but only two of the five would play that day.

To counteract the Eagles' pass rush early on, as well as the seven defensive backs they were using, Malzahn elected early in the first half to rely on the Bulldogs' ground game. It was a move that paid off to the tune of 207 yards rushing on 42 carries, a 4.9-yard average, highlighted by a 119-yard rushing performance by Matt Clinkscales. It wasn't quite as sexy as the 38–14 win by Springdale the year before over Evangel — a game in which Mustain threw for 266 yards and accounted for four touchdowns — but a win was a win in Malzahn's eyes.

Despite the average statistical performance, Mustain managed a few highlights, particularly a 48-yard pass down the middle to Damian Williams in the first quarter. The catch was one of four for Williams, who scored his only touchdown on one of his five rushes, sprinting 25 yards on the Bulldogs' first drive. Williams' performance stood out to the Fox Sports audience, including the men who were waiting to see Springdale six days later at Prescott.

"Did anybody see them on TV last week?" one man asked the group.

"Yeah, that kid who is going to Florida (Williams) was something else," another responded. "We've got to find a way to get him (to Arkansas)."

To their left, Springdale's players began making their way through the crowd, across the track and onto the field for warmups. They took the field for their pregame stretching in orderly precision behind the lead of senior Russ Greenlee. It was Greenlee who wore the black Nike armband around a belt loop on his pants, a symbol of the leader of the defense and a tradition started by the players while Jarrell Williams still coached.

The armband had been passed to Greenlee in the moments following the Little Rock Central loss the season before by outgoing senior linebacker Zach Pruitt. The decision to give the symbol to a player with the small stature of Greenlee, a 5-foot-10, 182-pound cornerback whose game was speed and playmaking, wasn't one Pruitt made lightly. The armband had traditionally stayed with one of the defense's larger players, either on the line or linebacker, and the player who wore it was normally the defense's most vocal leader, something Greenlee was anything but.

Chase Davis, an undersized linebacker with a mean streak to make up for his lack of size, was the player the Springdale coaches looked to lead the defense in 2005, and he was the player Pruitt had most considered other than Greenlee for the armband. However, Greenlee had both performance and tradition on his side. Not only had he started — and played well — for the Bulldogs since he was a sophomore, but his name also carried with it a legacy of its own in Springdale because his father, Doug Greenlee, had been the quarterback on the 1982 state championship team.

The circus-like atmosphere surrounding the recruitment of The Springdale Five over the summer had worn on Greenlee, as had the expectations that came with being the bearer of the armband. He had garnered some recruiting attention of his own from smaller colleges, but the constant media attention and pressure surrounding the upcoming season — as well as all his time on the field over the past three years — had left him burned out on the game he used to play for fun. Now his enjoyment came on the baseball diamond, where he started at second base for Springdale and had set a school record for home runs as a junior.

He had watched as Mustain had drawn a lot of media attention, a position he didn't envy.

"If I was him and I had the chance to play football at any major college or go to Harvard, I'd go to Harvard," Greenlee said. "I'd leave and forget about all this crap and get on living a normal life."

As the Bulldog players followed Greenlee onto the field, the group of men who had staked out their positions nearly two hours earlier looked for specific players after finding their numbers in the program.

"There goes Mustain," one said, his right arm raised as he pointed toward the field.

"There's Webb, the one who's going to Notre Dame," another said, referring to offensive lineman Bartley Webb.

The group continued watching as the Bulldogs formed their lines, five yards apart, and went through a series of stretches. A few minutes later the first-team offense lined up in a spread formation, preparing to practice a few timing plays. The men watched in silence as Mustain's first few passes zipped through the predusk night. Finally, after a hard-thrown ball found its way into the hands of Andrew Norman, the man standing to the right of the three couldn't hold back.

"Oh my gosh," he said. "He could start for Arkansas right now."

None in the crowd before the Prescott game had any illusion regarding the outcome. Whereas the Bulldogs were ranked No. 1 in Arkansas, ranked nationally and played in the state's largest classification — and toughest conference — Prescott was two classes below, with less than 300 students in its high school, some 2,100 less than Springdale High.

Some in the crowd wondered aloud why such a mismatch was scheduled. As the story goes, in 2004, Malzahn thought the Bulldogs were set to play one of their three non-conference games against Tulsa power Jenks High School. Many other teams had finalized their schedules when Jenks backed out to play a more highly regarded team in Texas, and that left Malzahn in a pinch, a problem he solved with a phone call to Prescott coach Greg Smith.

The two coaches had attended Henderson State University in Arkadelphia, Arkansas, at the same time and had coached against each other in the eastern part of the state. Malzahn used that relationship to initiate the discussion. Smith agreed to the game, hoping to prepare his team for the playoffs and give his quarterback, A.J. Lewis, the opportunity for extra media attention and possibly a scholarship.

Prescott entered the 2004 contest fresh from playoff appearances in Smith's first two seasons, compiling a 21–5 record along the way. The Curley Wolves suited up 38 players, compared to 76 varsity players – sophomores not included — for the Bulldogs. Lewis' winding 66-yard touchdown run gave Prescott the early lead, but the Bulldogs followed with 44 unanswered points. Mustain completed all six of his passes in the first half, including three for touchdowns, in the 44–13 victory.

Lewis injured a knee a couple of weeks later and his loss sent Prescott into a tailspin. After a 2–1 start in 2004, Prescott won just one more game the rest of the season and missed the playoffs for the first time under Smith. It had also lost its 2005 season opener.

Smith's attitude the week leading up to the game was all positive, focusing not only on how talented the Bulldogs were but also the proud community of Prescott. He was genuinely excited for the people of the town to have a chance to host such an event

"We're proud of how we do things around here," he said. "And we like to showcase what we do in southwest Arkansas."

Up in the press box above the home bleachers before the game, one of Smith's bosses, Prescott assistant principal David Maxwell, also shared his thoughts on the event. Maxwell was helping prepare the box for that night's use as Springdale walked off the field after completing its warmup routine.

"They've got some big ole boys up north, don't they," Maxwell said. "They grow 'em big up there, and they've got a lot of them, that's the thing."

Maxwell went on to say the largest crowd Cummins Field had ever seen was a playoff game 10 years earlier when 4,500 people had packed the stadium, lining the track that circled around the field. Looking out at the crowd, he guessed that more than 2,000 had already arrived that night, with more still filing in.

"That's why we signed the contract — the gate," Maxwell said. "I mean, look at all of them; look at all the people."

Short on suspense, the game was crammed with Springdale highlights. After winning the coin flip, Malzahn elected to receive — a tactic he always used to set the tone. The Bulldogs needed just three plays to cover 69 yards for a touchdown. The drive took only 32 seconds and it began with a pair of deep completions to the opposite sidelines by Mustain. On the third play, Williams faked as though he was going to the sideline and then turned upfield, leaving his defender behind him. The pass was slightly overthrown, but Williams was able to haul it in, firmly planting his right foot in bounds before he ran out of the end zone.

Prescott's game plan then became obvious on its first offensive possession. After huddling with his teammates between each play, Curley Wolves' quarterback Ben Smith watched the 25-second clock before calling for the snap at the last second. Greg Smith knew the only way to stop Springdale's offense was to keep the ball away, and the only way to do that was for Prescott to hold it as long as possible.

The plan worked to perfection in the first quarter, during which the Curley Wolves held the ball for 10 minutes, 57 seconds out of the 12 minutes in the quarter. Springdale led 14–0, but the Bulldogs had run just seven plays, and Mustain and the offense had spent the majority of the game watching. Prescott's offense converted on several key third downs, and one fourth down at its own 29 to keep possession.

After a pair of 15-yard penalties against the Bulldogs, the Curley Wolves even managed to score early in the second quarter on a 30-yard field goal. Much like a year before, when the long touchdown run by Lewis had spread the message loud and clear that Prescott wouldn't just lie down for Springdale, the Curley Wolves had made their mark by scoring — regardless of what happened from there on — and the cheers from the home crowd let the Bulldogs know just that.

The reaction was a well-deserved one for the Prescott players, but it was short-lived. On its next possession, following the field goal by Prescott, Springdale once again made quick work of the Curley Wolves' secondary. The Bulldogs went 80 yards in just three plays, and it was Williams who once again capped the effort, this time in even more spectacular fashion than his first touchdown. After catches by Matt Clinkscales and Norman moved Springdale down to the Prescott 32, Mustain threw a 7-yard pass to Williams on his left on the third play of the drive. Williams turned after catching the ball, only to see a defender waiting five yards away. He moved his head back and forth, turning his shoulders as well to give the appearance that he was turning to his right, only to suddenly use his left foot to plant and turn back outside to his left, leaving the defender flat on his stomach as he rushed past. He then sprinted as though he were heading on a straight line toward the end zone 20 yards away as a pair of Prescott defenders closed on him. However, just as he reached the 11, Williams quickly turned his body back toward the middle of the field, leaving the overpursuing defenders unable to stop while he finished the play by dashing to the middle of the field for his second touchdown of the game.

"He makes us coaches look good with plays like that," Malzahn said of the play. "Isn't that something?"

Williams' second touchdown made it 21–3. At that point, the Bulldogs had run 10 plays, all passes, and had possession for just two minutes. Mustain had thrown one incompletion and had completed nine for 236 yards and three touchdowns — all the while feeling barely any pressure from the overmatched Prescott defense.

The Curley Wolves kept the ball for more than six minutes following Williams' score, but managed only 31 yards before punting. Norman returned it 29 to the Springdale 47. A 26-yard completion from Mustain to Zack Pianalto and a 27-yarder to Ben Cleveland and the lead was 28–3 with 1:52 left in the half.

Prescott was unable to get a first down following the Cleveland touchdown, and a 2-yard punt gave Springdale the ball back at the Curley Wolves' 24 with 1:27 left in the half. Two plays later, following one of Mustain's two incompletions in the half, the Bulldogs went up 34–3 when Clinkscales took a short screen pass and followed a wall — namely Webb and senior guard Allen Reed — into the end zone.

Mustain and the first-team offense were through and the numbers were incredible. Mustain completed 12 of 14 for 317 yards and five touchdowns. The passes were the only plays by the Bulldogs as they built a 31-point lead while holding the ball for just 2:28. Springdale's first running play occurred midway through the third quarter of the 46–3 win after the Bulldogs had secured the 35-point mercy-rule margin. Put in place a year earlier, the rule was intended to promote good sportsmanship and prevent blowouts by running the clock continuously when one team led by 35 or more in the second half. It was a rule Springdale had invoked ten times the season before with Evangel, their conference rival, Fort Smith Northside and Little Rock Central being the exceptions.

In his two games against the Curley Wolves, Mustain completed 18 of 20 for 484 yards and eight touchdowns in less than four full quarters. His presence, and his future with the Razorbacks, had been the reason for many of the people to come and watch Springdale, and despite the lopsided score in the second half, few left the stadium early. The reason became clear just minutes after the game ended.

As Mustain shook hands with several Prescott players, people gathered on the field by the home sideline. More entered the field each minute, all of them waiting for a chance to meet him.

By the time Mustain noticed the crowd, over 200 people were waiting on him, while several had already pulled aside Williams, asking for his autograph. Once he completed a series of interviews, Mustain was astonished to see several children with footballs waiting for him to do the same. An equal number of adults soon followed, keeping Mustain on the field for nearly an hour after the game ended.

The people of Prescott had gotten the show they wanted and a piece of the superstars they had heard so much about. Mustain had been down this road before, with the greetings in the hallway at school from classmates he didn't know during his junior year. It had all been very strange, as had the autograph seekers, yet the experience had been a fun one.

"I don't mind it," he said. "It's kind of fun really."

Webb wasn't quite as kind in his assessment of the evening for the first teamers as the Bulldogs prepared for the long drive home.

"We drove 4½ hours for 14 plays," he said.

"Fourteen plays, can you believe that?"

CHAPTER 9
Battle of the Bulldogs

THE FIRST PEOPLE CLAIMED THEIR SEATS AT HARMON FIELD AT 4:30 IN THE AFTERNOON, MORE THAN THREE HOURS BEFORE KICKOFF. They did so by placing blankets on sections of the bleacher seats on the visitors' side of the field before leaving to find pregame conversation elsewhere around the campus of Fayetteville High.

Large crowds were the norm anytime Fayetteville and Springdale faced each other on the football field, but tonight was anything but normal. It was the Battle of the Bulldogs, the annual rivalry game between the neighboring Washington County foes. Only this time it was between the top two ranked teams in Arkansas — the first time the two had met as No. 1 and No. 2 since 1984.

Springdale entered the game even more solidified as the team to beat in Arkansas after its 44–0 win over Jenks, Oklahoma, two weeks before, and an easy 41–3 win in its conference opener against Fort Smith Southside the week earlier. The Bulldogs' win against Jenks came on the heels of their win at Prescott, and was the second nationally televised game for Springdale in the team's first three weeks.

Both the Bulldogs and Jenks were ranked nationally when they faced off on ESPNU. Coming off an emotional victory over rival Tulsa Union, Jenks was not prepared for Springdale. Particularly, the Trojans were not prepared for Damian Williams.

He made a shambles of Jenks' secondary, catching three first-half touchdown passes from Mitch Mustain as the Bulldogs built a 30–0 lead. He finished with nine catches for 147 yards and a school-record four TDs, prompting Jenks coach Allan Trimble to call Williams "one of the most gifted athletes I've ever seen." Despite playing in only nine quarters, Williams had accounted for seven touchdowns in three games.

Williams' ability on the football field had been on the radar for the coaches at Springdale High since even before Gus Malzahn had been hired as the head coach. His athleticism combined with the abilities to stop and start suddenly — leaving opponents off balance as he rushed past them — and to simply outrun those trying to guard him were second to none. He was the one athlete the coaches knew could score from anyplace on the field, something he had done often during his days at Central Junior High and as a sophomore playing on the varsity team.

Williams was a sophomore when he began making an impact, both as a running back and receiver. However, his season ended after an awkward hit while trying to get into the end zone. After the play, Williams lay on the field, unable to move anything but his head.

He had suffered a chipped vertebra in his neck, caused by the hit and a smaller than normal spinal canal. Paralyzed for a while, he awoke suddenly at the hospital and realized he could move his arms.

"That was one of the happiest moments of my life," he said. "I was so scared that I wasn't going to be able to walk again."

Even after recovering his movement, Williams faced a long and grueling rehabilitation process. A couple of doctors told him playing football was no longer an option, even with rehabilitation, but Williams would have none of it. Instead, he spent several months working to strengthen his neck and shoulders in anticipation of his next big hit.

The work paid off for Williams as he returned for his junior season, his talent on offense and defense leading to a scholarship offer from the University of Arkansas — the third member of the Springdale Five to be offered by the Razorbacks. In his junior year, he logged playing time in the secondary and returning kickoffs, in addition to playing running back and receiver.

As good as Williams was as a junior — good enough to bring in more than 20 scholarship offers following the season — his performance was once again hindered somewhat by injury. He missed several games during the middle of the season after suffering a sprained ankle on a punt return against Fayetteville. Even before that his sometimes tentative play on offense left some of his coaches wondering if he had completely conquered the lingering thoughts of his neck injury from the season before.

For Williams, the most telling moment of the season came in the loss to Little Rock Central in the state semifinals. With Springdale trailing in the second quarter, Williams caught a screen pass from Mustain and turned up field. Before he could get started, a defender firmly planted his helmet in Williams' arm and chest. The tackle left Williams momentarily dazed, lying face down in the churned-up turf. He slowly got to his feet and tried to catch his breath. Williams dropped another pass as a defender closed in and it wasn't until he made a leaping catch in the second half that he seemed back on his game.

His performance left the Central coaches wondering aloud afterward if Williams had quit on his team following the early deficit and big hit. There had already been doubts from his own coaches and teammates about Williams' attitude during the season, prompted by a seemingly selfish demeanor and moments such as when he walked into the fieldhouse wearing flashy sunglasses. Whether the doubts were justified or not were up for debate since Williams wasn't as open as some of the others about his life away from football, but they were there nevertheless. Some of the mistrust likely came because of his status as the only black player to start for Springdale that season, as well as being enveloped in the circle of jealously and resentment that a few of the seniors felt toward Williams and the rest of the junior class for the considerable attention they were receiving in the media.

More than anything, what Williams' junior season did was make him aware that he needed to do more if he was going to fulfill all the expectations — his own first and foremost. To that end, he quit the baseball team during the spring as the college recruiters began showing more and more attention, preferring to spend his practice time on the football field and in the weight room. He added 10 pounds of muscle, bulking up to 188 pounds, his neck injury no longer an issue.

"I knew I had to change something," Williams said. "I played well (as a junior), but not to the extent to which I'm capable of."

He was also acutely aware of the impact his perceived me-first attitude had on his teammates the season before, something he set out to change as a senior. He did so by refusing to talk about himself to reporters after games, no matter how many times the questions about spectacular play were asked. He would give credit to his offensive linemen, the blocks by his receivers, Mustain . . . anything but his own play. It was a plainly calculated move by Williams, but it was one appreciated by even those who had questioned his commitment to the team the season before.

"I've taken a different perspective on things this year," Williams said. "Last year it was kind of about me.

"I've never really been a selfish person, but I think this year I've realized it is more about the team and it's more that your team stays together and complements each other so we have a stronger bond."

During the spring and summer Williams kept his thoughts on the schools who were recruiting him mostly to himself. He didn't share his pros and cons on each of the schools until surprising many with his commitment to Florida the first week of two-a-day practices in August. The mystery surrounding his choice led many to speculate about his reasons for leaving Arkansas. When he did share some of what he was thinking, it sounded as though he didn't feel like the Razorbacks coaching staff and fans had shown him as much attention as Mustain and the other Springdale players during the recruiting process, a fact which rankled him.

"I decided I had to come out here and had to prove myself to the state of Arkansas," Williams said while talking of his quick start to the season. "You hear people say, 'He's not as good as they're saying he is' and all this stuff.

"I wanted to be the person that lives up to the hype that we got."

Living up to the hype was just what Williams did through the first four games, averaging five catches and 106 yards receiving per contest. With his four touchdown catches against Jenks and another the following week against Fort Smith Southside, his total was at seven. Also, he had rushed for 133 yards — nearly reaching his total for the season before — on just seven carries, an average of 19 yards every time he ran with the ball.

"We may be watching one of the better athletes to come around in a while," Malzahn said.

• • •

Fayetteville and Springdale first met on the football field in 1908 when the towns were miles apart and most people traveled by horse and wagon.

As they prepared for the 106th meeting in the fall of 2005, the farmland once separating the two had disappeared. Their border was a seamless blend of commercial and residential development.

The two high schools also shared the same mascot, a Bulldog — hence the nickname for the game. Each had carved out its own identity of the Bulldog over the years by using school colors to differentiate from their neighboring rival. For Fayetteville that meant being called the Purple

'Dogs more often than not by its alumni and students, while Springdale went by the Red 'Dogs when it came time to square off with the folks from the south.

While the two shared much in common — and had benefited from the rapid growth in Northwest Arkansas over the past decade to the point that their combined population had surged past 100,000 — the cities could not have been farther apart in the makeup of their residents. No matter how many people moved in, people in the two cities continued to have a distrust for one another.

As a 1981 graduate of Fayetteville, Rick Doss knew the rivalry well as his son, Travis, prepared to suit out for the final time in the rivalry in 2004 — for Springdale. Travis was the starting center for the Red 'Dogs as a senior, something Rick never could have imagined in his Purple 'Dog days.

Back then, Rick bled purple as a member of the Fayetteville football team. Like many of his teammates and members of the community, beating Springdale was the most important game of the year, one that could make a losing season bearable.

Rick had grown up in Fayetteville, with the University of Arkansas and its academia at the core of its predominantly white-collar makeup. Many of his classmates prided themselves on what they perceived as a higher class of living, especially when compared to their neighbors to the north. In their eyes, Springdale would always be the little town that had grown from its agricultural beginnings, the rectangular chicken houses that dotted its landscape a constant reminder of what the town had been and always would be — "Chickendale."

Making matters worse for Springdale's reputation in the eyes of its rival was the presence of the headquarters of Tyson Foods. The company was founded in 1935 in Springdale, and despite growing into a worldwide economic force in the poultry industry, its name only fueled the fire for those wishing to take shots at Springdale. One of the classic Fayetteville student gags at both football and basketball games was to break out the large buckets from Kentucky Fried Chicken during games and wear them as hats. There was also the annual chicken dinner before games for many.

"I guess it's because Springdale is known as kind of redneck to the Fayetteville kids," Rick said of the reason for the rivalry. "They think we're blue-collar, cowboy kind of people because we've got the rodeo grounds here.

"And then you look at Fayetteville; I bet 70 percent of my class are lawyers now. Fayetteville's just a white-collar, coat-and-tie kind of place."

Now on the other side of the rivalry, Rick had no problem talking up the virtues of Springdale while talking down his childhood home. After leaving Northwest Arkansas to attend college and start a family, Rick had returned to Fayetteville briefly in the early '90s before moving to Springdale.

"Fayetteville's changed a lot since I left," Rick said. "Personally, I think Springdale's a better place to live, and it's friendlier."

His reference was to the college crowd in Fayetteville as well as a more liberal city government, one that had often made life difficult for developers with its strict building and environmental restrictions.

"All I see when I look at Fayetteville now is a bunch of tree huggers," he said.

As the two schools prepared for their 2005 meeting, the significance of the rivalry was as big as ever, but not only because of the No. 1 vs. No. 2 matchup that awaited. Also playing a large role for many of the alumni was a school not involved in the game — Springdale's newest high school, Har-Ber High.

Har-Ber had opened its doors in August with mostly sophomores, although a smattering of juniors and seniors had chosen to attend the new school as well. As for athletics, the state governing body of high school sports — the Arkansas Activities Association's Board of Directors — voted before the school year to allow Har-Ber to participate in all varsity sports before the season, all except football. So while Northwest Arkansas' newest high school prepared to begin varsity play in 2006 by fielding just a junior varsity team in 2005, fans across the area were already discussing the impact the school would have.

Most of the talk focused on just what Har-Ber's arrival would do to not only the Springdale-Fayetteville rivalry but also the likely rivalry between the two Springdale schools as well. Many in Springdale went out of their way to deny any rivalry would exist between the intra-city schools, focusing instead on the hope that only friendly competition would prevail. Others, however, were more realistic about what would happen, especially with the likely socioeconomic disparities between the two.

"Oh, there's no doubt that Springdale High and Har-Ber will be the number one rivalry," said Jarrell Williams, who upon being hired as head football coach at Springdale in 1965 had been told that defeating Fayetteville was "the most important thing every year."

"Of course, the Fayetteville rivalry will still be there," he continued. "But it will be almost secondary."

From Fayetteville's standpoint, one thought was that its rivalry would continue with the city of Springdale, regardless of how many high schools it had. It was a thought Fayetteville head coach Daryl Patton quickly dismissed.

"We don't care about Har-Ber," he said. "Springdale's our rival forever.

"Our philosophy, and I think everybody here feels the same way, is that they call it the Battle of the Bulldogs. Har-Ber is not the Bulldogs — they're going to be the Wildcats or whatever.

"Springdale's going to be our rivalry game. Next year, we're going to line up and play them and that's going to be our rivalry game."

All that said, Patton admitted there wouldn't likely be as much intensity for the Battle of the Bulldogs in the future, not with one fan base being split in two.

"But that's the game we're going to circle and get ready to play."

• • •

By the time kickoff came around at 7:30 on the night of the Battle of the Bulldogs, an overflow crowd had made its way into the stadium surrounding Harmon Field. Rumbling echoed throughout the hills around the valley in which the stadium sat, a reminder of the more than 300,000 motorcycle enthusiasts who had made their way to Fayetteville for an annual festival on the first weekend in October.

More than an hour before kickoff, the only unoccupied seats at Harmon Field were some chairbacks that belonged to those with season tickets to the Fayetteville games. Even they filled up 30 minutes before gametime. Included in that crowd was Arkansas head coach Houston Nutt, at the game to watch his son play quarterback for the Purple 'Dogs, and the five players he had offered from the Red 'Dogs.

More than 8,200 other fans sought out any viewing point. Some stood on the track in the south end zone, behind a temporary fence.

Others sat on the grassy embankments in the corners of the stadium. Anywhere to find a spot to watch.

For just a bit, Springdale appeared vulnerable. After going 79 yards on the opening drive — all running plays — for a 7–0 lead, the Red 'Dogs gave Fayetteville momentum with a pair of fumbles. The Purple 'Dogs managed to tie the game after the first turnover, but Springdale led 35–7 at the half.

Fayetteville opened the second half with a 79-yard TD drive, the longest of the season by a Springdale opponent. At 35–14, Damian Williams took over.

Outside of one key punt return, Williams had struggled in the first half, fumbling once and dropping a pass near the end zone. His response was to atone with one of his now-common performances. This time he caught his first pass from Mustain near the sideline and quickly turned back inside. As he sprinted toward the end zone, a pair of Fayetteville defenders appeared to have the proper angles, but he split them with a burst of speed on his way to a 65-yard touchdown.

The only suspense as the game entered the fourth quarter was how quickly could Springdale score to reach the 35-point mercy-rule margin needed to start the continuous clock. Williams answered that just 38 seconds into the quarter when he scored his second touchdown, a 22-yard run after a short pass over the middle from Mustain.

Springdale did get the ball back on offense one more time late in the fourth quarter, and following his usual precedent, Malzahn took out the first-team offense with the Red 'Dogs up by 35. What he didn't count on was the second teamers driving deep into Fayetteville territory. With less than two minutes remaining and Springdale driving, Malzahn turned to his assistants and asked if he should try to score another touchdown. He had called all running plays on the drive so far to give Fayetteville every chance to stop the attack, but the Bulldogs had nevertheless made their way down the field behind Matt Clinkscales' backup, senior Adam Jones.

Malzahn's assistants, minus longtime defensive assistant Kerry Winberry, all voted to go for another score. The point the other assistants made was that a week earlier against Fort Smith Southside, Jones had a chance at a late touchdown before Malzahn elected to kneel on the final few snaps, allowing the clock to run out. They wanted to reward Jones for his effort against Fayetteville, but Winberry knew the history of the rivalry and thought the Purple 'Dog faithful would perceive another touchdown as running up the score.

Jones did score with less than a minute remaining to stretch the final score to 56–14, and just as Winberry had guessed, several in the Fayetteville crowd booed the touchdown.

"Sure looks like greed to me," one fan said. "And greed always comes back to get you."

Patton said afterward he had no problem with the final Springdale touchdown, insisting it was the Purple 'Dogs' job to stop its opponent. After some time to think about Jones' score, Winberry agreed.

"You don't tell the kids not to do their best," Winberry said.

Mitch Mustain is led off the field by trainers Jamie Croley (left) and Chad Fink (right) on November 26, 2004. Mustain suffered a broken arm moments earlier during the second quarter of Springdale High's state semifinal game with Little Rock Central.

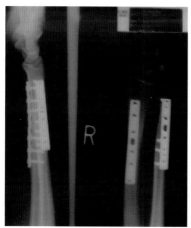

X-rays of Mitch Mustain's broken right arm following more than three hours of surgery. Steel plates were attached to help with healing and Mustain was told he wouldn't be able to participate in contact sports for between 3–6 months.

The hurt of a devastating loss to Little Rock Central in 2004 came down hard on the Springdale seniors such as defensive lineman Nathan Bull.

Andrew Norman, star of the Nike® 7-on-7 Passing Championship in Los Angeles.

One Year, One Team, One Goal . . . the motto of the 2005 Bulldogs, shown here after a game at the Southeast Select 7-on-7 Tournament in Hoover, Alabama, in July.

Five straight games in the oppressive Alabama heat proved to be too much for Springdale in Hoover. Three players were taken to a local hospital following the tournament, including Ryan Hoover (left) and Mason Price (right).

Sometimes frustrated at his perceived stereotype as a possession receiver, Andrew Norman proves otherwise against future University of Georgia cornerback Prince Miller at Hoover.

Television stations from across Arkansas made their way to Springdale on August 15, 2005 for the announcement that Mitch Mustain and Andrew Norman would be Razorbacks.

Bulldogs coach Gus Malzahn spent much of the summer of 2005 trying to avoid too much attention for The Springale Five, but even he couldn't stop this picture of the talented players together with their coach after Mustain and Norman's announcement. Top row (left to right): Mitch Mustain, Gus Malzahn and Andrew Norman. Bottom row: Bartley Webb, Damian Williams and Ben Cleveland.

Displaying his usual picture-perfect form, and with his initial commitment to the University of Arkansas behind him, Mitch Mustain delivers a pass during a preseason scrimmage.

After a hectic summer schedule, full of 7-on-7 action and recruiting buzz, the Bulldogs finally got back to business on the field against Evangel Christian at the Independence Bowl in Shreveport, Louisiana.

Damian Williams wasted little time in setting the tone for his spectacular 2005 season with a stellar effort against Evangel Christian from Shreveport, Louisiana.

Leading the way in Springdale's win on national television was senior running back Matt Clinkscales, not one of The Springdale Five but an emotional leader for the Bulldogs.

The people of Prescott came to see what all the fuss about the boys from Springdale was all about . . . and to meet a few rising stars.

Chase Davis, here making a tackle against Fayetteville, wasn't the biggest or most recruited of the Bulldogs, but he was the heartbeat of the team.

Mitch Mustain takes a moment following Springdale's win over Fort Smith Northside to show Gus Malzahn's age at a birthday party for the coach.

Quarterback and coach discuss strategy, something not often needed as the Bulldogs steamrolled their opponents in 2005.

Even as she enjoyed senior night with her son before the regular-season finale, Beck Campbell knew his college future was very much in question.

The weekly signing sessions after games weren't reserved for only Mitch Mustain, as evidenced here by the crowd around Damian Williams.

As the season continued, the crowds continued to grow at Jarrell Williams Bulldog Stadium, shown behind junior standout Zack Pianalto.

Gus Malzahn looks for just the right song in a lighter moment on the Bulldogs bus ride to Little Rock for the state championship game. In the back of the bus, Malzahn's players discuss the future of their coach.

The game on the field shows little of the soft side of Ben Cleveland. Here, the gentle giant helps 2-year-old Caylea Clark of Mountain Home, Arkansas, put together a puzzle during a visit by 15 members of the Bulldogs to Arkansas Children's Hospital the day before the championship game.

Always looking to keep his players focused, Gus Malzahn puts the Bulldogs through an early morning workout the day of the championship game.

Russ Greenlee looks for some quiet time in the moments leading up to the championship game.

Usually one to rely on preparation over emotion, Gus Malzahn reminds the Bulldogs of the importance of completing their mission.

MICHAEL ZAMORA

Andrew Norman (2), Aaron Finch (44), Damian Williams (1) and Mitch Mustain (16) hold hands on their way out of the tunnel and into War Memorial Stadium.

MICHAEL ZAMORA

*More than 25,000 officially filed into War Memorial Stadium for Springdale's
championship game against West Memphis, though most observers estimated the
crowd at nearer to 35,000. Here, the crowd is shown in the first half while many
were still in lines outside the stadium waiting to enter.*

West Memphis players line up on the field for the pregame coin toss, seemingly facing all of Springdale.

TOM EWART

Before he left Arkansas for Notre Dame, Bartley Webb took time to enjoy the fruits of the Bulldog's labor following their 54–20 win over West Memphis.

MICHAEL ZAMORA

TOM EWART

The people of Springdale had more than just a state championship on their thoughts as the 2005 season wound down.

MICHAEL ZAMORA

Even with their season completed, Mitch Mustain, Andrew Norman and Damian Williams were still the talk of Arkansas. Here, the players watch as 8-year-old Jaylen Bell of Rogers dances in a mirror as the three take Bell shopping at a Wal-Mart Supercenter in Springdale. Tyson employees raffled off an autographed Springdale football to raise money to buy a bike for Bell, who suffers from tubular sclerosis. The three football players used the remaining money to buy gifts for Bell and his family, including the mirror, after noticing how much Bell enjoyed watching himself dance.

CHAPTER 10
Home of the Mercy Rule

BEVERLY MARVEGGIO DIDN'T KNOW EXACTLY WHY SHE WAS SO DRAWN TO THE PASSION SURROUNDING ATHLETICS, BUT IT WASN'T SOMETHING SHE THOUGHT ABOUT ALL THAT OFTEN. Instead, she spent much of her energy teaching that passion to her daughter, Kyla, and younger son, Derek.

Bev believed that competing hard and playing games with respect for those who played them was a way for her children to learn about life, and not just in terms of on the field or court. Winning and losing was secondary — though winning was preferred — to playing the right way.

Her lessons to her children began at an early age. For Derek, that meant taking part in his first organized football as a first-grader. The flag football variety of the game wasn't nearly as physical as the impromptu wrestling matches with his mom at home, and even then he knew the game was something his mother took seriously.

"She was meaner than any linebacker I've seen in the NFL, I can tell you that," Derek said. "She made (Baltimore Ravens star linebacker) Ray Lewis look like a little puppy dog."

The summer before his fourth-grade year, the lessons meant making the 25-minute drive each weekday from their home in Siloam Springs on the Arkansas-Oklahoma border to Springdale. They made the trips to the weeklong Springdale Bulldog football camp so Derek could participate and she could watch.

Derek was the only camper at the event not from Springdale, but that was of little significance to Bev. She knew Jarrell Williams' twin brother, Darrell, from their time working together in the Siloam Springs school district, and she was well aware of the winning tradition in Springdale under Jarrell. Her respect for the coach was such that after dropping Derek off for the camp each day, she would watch from the stands as her son impressed the Bulldogs' coaches with his instinctive nose for the football. After the day's work was done, the two would drive back home to Siloam Springs and ready themselves for the next day's trip.

While watching Derek at the camp, Bev often kept quiet up in the stands. That wasn't the case, however, when it came time for either Derek or Kyla to compete. Her "holler," as husband Brad called it, was such that "everyone around would hear and know it was her," and it was a constant reminder to her children to give their all.

As Derek entered the seventh grade in Siloam Springs in the fall of 2000, he did so as a quarterback on the middle school football team. It was during a game that season that he injured a leg, an injury not serious but enough to cause him to leave during the second half. While standing on the sidelines, watching his teammates go on without him, Derek grew bored with the action and was ready to rest. So he took off his helmet and slipped off his shoulder pads.

Bev couldn't believe what she was seeing. She had taught her son better, and after a quiet drive home that night, she let him know it once they walked into the house.

"You never take your pads off unless you're seriously hurt," she told Derek during the scolding. "Never."

The one-way conversation lasted more than 10 minutes before Brad came home. He was a pilot and had missed the game while flying, but within seconds of walking in the house he knew his wife was all business.

"She was letting him have it," he said. "I mean, she was right up in his face."

Bev's message hit home with a frightened and impressionable Derek.

"It was scary," Derek said. "I never did that again, I can tell you that."

It was shortly after the incident with the pads that fall that Bev's infamous holler began to quiet somewhat. She was feeling weak and ill much of the time, leading to a doctor's visit shortly before Christmas. That was where she learned of her illness — cervical cancer.

Brad was in Tulsa on business when he received the call from his wife. He struggled to remain standing when she told him the news. He was so shaken that he was unable to pilot the plane home, something a co-worker did for him.

Derek had no idea of his mother's illness or that she had gone to the doctor when he and his sister arrived home that afternoon after school. He knew something was awry, however, when they walked in and his minister was there with his mom and dad. The three calmly, yet firmly, delivered the news of Bev's cancer to Derek and Kyla.

"We didn't know how to take it," Derek said. "She was fine at the time, but we knew it was serious business."

It was only a few weeks later that Bev started treatment for the cancer in Houston. She and Brad rented a small apartment there from December through March while Derek and Kyla remained with their grandparents in Siloam Springs — traveling back and forth to see their parents.

It was early during their stay in Houston that a tired Bev — worn down from the chemotherapy — asked Brad one evening to wash her hair for her. He did so softly and peacefully, only to have his eyes open wide when he realized some of her hair remained on his fingers after he pulled them away. The side effect of the treatment was a common and expected one, but nevertheless Bev struggled with the sight — breaking down in tears.

The sight of his wife — admittedly the stronger emotionally of the pair — in tears was too much for him to handle. The next morning, Brad wasted little time before finding a beautician who specialized in making wigs for cancer patients.

"It was the best thing that I did," he said.

Soon after returning to Siloam Springs from Houston that spring, Bev began feeling better and doctors told her the cancer had gone into remission. Throughout that summer, the family tried to return to normal, which for Derek meant going out for eighth-grade football. He was the backup quarterback that season, getting his chance to play a full game around Thanksgiving when the starter was out with a cold.

In the weeks leading up to the game, Bev started feeling worse than during the initial onset of her cancer. She had not yet been rediagnosed, but the symptoms were there — and both she and Brad knew it.

When Derek told her that he would start that night against Shiloh Christian, Bev decided that no matter the pain she would go. Brad was out of town working, so she drove herself to the game — parking outside the fence that lined the field and positioning herself so she could watch her son help his team win the game.

The game would be her last.

"You could tell she wasn't feeling well," Brad said. "I'll never forget I called home and she was so excited. She said, 'I made it to the game, and I got to watch Derek play.'"

Bev Marveggio died April 21, 2002, at the age of 46. Her death came after a 16-month battle — the last two-and-a-half weeks of which were spent in a coma. Her passion in life had served as an example of how to live for her children, and her strength in the face of death had taught them a lesson they'd never forget.

"She always taught me to be a fighter, and I never saw the cancer once get her down," Derek said. "She fought until the very end."

• • •

If you were to ask Derek Marveggio to name his favorite place, it would be somewhere deep in the woods, away from everything civilized and modern.

It was there — while on his weekend hunting trips — that Marveggio was most at peace in his young life. It was there, surrounded by the quiet sounds of nature, he had spent much of the three-and-a-half years since his mother's death — searching for his own answers while avoiding the questions.

Derek's dad, Brad, had wanted to ask his son about his feelings following the death of Beverly, but he wasn't sure how to approach the conversation — at least not without losing control of his emotions that he worked so hard to keep under control.

Following Bev's death, Brad quickly made the decision to move his family from Siloam Springs to Springdale. That was where his job was and after marrying Trish in December of 2002, he thought a change of scenery would be good for him and his children as they all continued to cope with their loss.

Kyla stayed in Siloam Springs for her final year of high school, living with an aunt. Derek moved with his dad to their new home in Tontitown, just west of Springdale, and finished his ninth-grade year at Southwest Junior High. He got along fine with Trish, but he was still dealing with the loss of his mom and moving to a new school. He told his dad he was thinking about giving up football as a sophomore, but his mother's passion for the game made the decision difficult.

When he shared his thoughts about not playing with his dad, Brad didn't react well. He suspected that Derek didn't want to play because of thoughts of his mother, but that was exactly why he thought Derek needed to play.

"He thought I was forcing him, but really I was just encouraging him," Brad said. "I just told him, 'No, you need to play.'"

Derek soon appreciated his dad's advice. The Springdale sophomore team — led by quarterback Mitch Mustain — finished the season 10–0. Derek played linebacker and soon began to realize he was playing for more than just himself. He was honoring his mother's memory, even if he didn't know how to say it at the time.

"I bet she's just jumping for joy because she got her wish," Derek later said of his mom's desire for him to play at Springdale. "And she still gets to see me play."

Derek was in the same situation as many other 11th graders at Springdale. Talented enough to play at other schools in the area, their playing time was limited on a team loaded with stars. Late in the season, the 5-foot-10, 165-pounder tore a ligament in one of his knees, and he was on crutches when Springdale fell to Little Rock Central in the semifinals of the playoffs.

Making things worse during the offseason that followed, he recovered slowly. He had hoped hard work would mean more playing time as a senior, but his running and lifting were limited, and his dreams were fading.

"Everyone was getting bigger and faster, and I was getting smaller and slower," he said.

Derek began his senior season on the sidelines, only entering games when the Bulldogs had reached the 35-point mercy rule during the second half and after Gus Malzahn pulled the starters. The outcome of games was never in question when he entered, but he played hard nevertheless — without even a hint of animosity for those starting ahead of him.

Whereas pride might have caused some in the same situation to sulk about what might have been, Derek instead put all his energy into his limited time on the field and helping those around him succeed. One way he did so was by helping the coaches while on the bench — signaling in the defensive play calls from the sidelines. It was a small role, one which a younger player might normally fill, but it was something Derek's coaches noticed and respected.

He didn't set out to become such an active emotional leader; it just happened. Sending in the plays was something he had asked to do only as a way to stay "in the game," when his time did come.

"I could be sitting over there shooting the bull with my friends, but it helps me for when I go out there because I've seen all the plays for two or three quarters," he said.

But the image of a senior sending in plays from the sidelines was one several of his teammates and coaches saw as symbolic. If Derek didn't complain, then how could they?

"A lot of seniors would just sulk and say, 'No way am I doing that,'" Dennis DeBusk said. "But Derek's the ultimate team player."

His reward wasn't a college scholarship or the adoration of the masses. Instead, it was knowing that he was living up to the expectations of his mother.

During the win over Jenks, Oklahoma, Derek entered the game in the fourth quarter and promptly made a tackle. He realized, "I had just made a tackle on national television," and thought about the source of his aggressive nature.

"She was always telling me to go out and play hard, and I can feel her when I hit somebody," he said of his mother. "Or when I get blocked and I'm not really trying to get off (the block).

"I know she's there saying 'What the crud are you doing?'"

Fortunately for Derek, and many of the other second-teamers, the first five games provided plenty of playing time. He saw action in each of the five games, including the entire second half against Prescott.

And each and every time he stepped on the field, Derek kept his mother in his thoughts.

"My mom was always like, 'I'd give anything for you to play for Springdale,'" he said. "She got her wish.

"She's got the greatest seat in the house, and I know she's up there."

• • •

A clock hanging on the wall above where Kathy Hardin, Malzahn's secretary, sat on the upper level of the Springdale fieldhouse read "Home of the mercy rule" in homage to Springdale's 10 such wins during 2004. As the second half of the regular season in 2005 began, the Bulldogs already had five such wins under their belt in as many games.

The wins, however, were the least of their concerns.

Following the win over Fayetteville, Springdale's march through its conference continued with a 56–21 win at Russellville, nearly an hour bus ride down Interstate-540 and another hour on I-40. During the summer, several in Russellville began looking forward to the game, including the cook in a popular local restaurant who asked aloud whether the game was home or away. Told the game was in Russellville, the cook smiled and said, "You can bet I'll be there for that one."

He likely was there on October 7 — along with the rest that came to see Mitch Mustain and the Bulldogs. Once play began, the game became a good old-fashioned gunslinger battle between Mustain and another of the state's top quarterbacks, Eli Cranor. They threw for a total of 500 yards in the first half, with Mustain completing all but two of his 20.

Away from the field, however, not all was well with the Bulldogs as they made the trek home. In the weeks leading up to the Russellville game, Robert Norman — Andrew's father — began noticing that the timing on certain routes was seemingly off between his son and Mustain. There had been several passes from Mustain during the Fayetteville game which hadn't found their mark, and despite a three-touchdown performance at Russellville, Robert was wondering to those around him if there was a problem between Andrew and Mitch.

Several around and on the team speculated the reason for Robert's concern had nothing to do with Andrew's play on the field. He was just one off the team lead for catches, but his three touchdown catches lagged behind the nine by Damian Williams. One coach suggested that the root of all Robert's problems was the breakout season Williams was having, overshadowing much of Andrew's success. Robert had always been tough on Andrew, often critiquing his performances and comparing them to his own playing days, but his latest concerns had several coaches worrying they might be impacting Andrew's performance.

"Andrew's not the problem, and he's never been," the coach said. "He's just hearing this crap at home and it's getting in his head."

Robert's tension boiled over the week following the Russellville game when Springdale hosted Bentonville. Andrew and Mitch were off on several passes during the 42–14 win by the Bulldogs, a game Andrew finished with just two catches for 28 yards. That compared to four catches for 153 yards and four more touchdowns by Williams, including a pair of jaw-dropping touchdown catches when he left opposing defenders grabbing at air as he whisked past.

During the game, Robert could be heard in the crowd venting his frustrations. Afterward, he confronted volunteer assistant coach Rhett Lashlee, again asking what the problem was between his son and Mustain. Lashlee, who had been a three-year starting quarterback in high school at Shiloh Christian and later played at the University of Arkansas, didn't react well to the suggestion that Andrew was struggling, or that Mustain's timing was off. He insisted to Robert that the only thing that mattered was the fact Springdale had just won the game. But Robert would have none of it. He was sure there was a problem between Andrew and Mitch and he wanted details.

Quietly during the following week, Malzahn put an end to any further outbursts. In keeping with his usual mode of operation, Malzahn would not discuss the incident either publicly or privately, but that didn't keep other coaches from speculating about what the head coach was thinking.

"You watch this week (against Van Buren)," one said. "Norman's going to get the ball the entire way down the field on that first series, and we're not going to hear about any more problems."

Sure enough, on the first play against the Pointers, Andrew got the ball on a double reverse, running 48 yards. He finished the drive on the next play, a 5-yard touchdown catch in the corner of the end zone. He went on to finish with 109 yards receiving on four catches, one of five receivers to catch the six touchdown passes by Mustain in the 42–7 win.

"That should take care of that," the coach said.

Also in that game, another incident popped up when running back Matt Clinkscales — upset at not receiving any carries in the game — threw his helmet to the ground on the sidelines, voicing his frustration loud enough for all to hear. It was the second time in seven games that Clinkscales hadn't gotten a carry in a game (Prescott being the other), both instances only adding fuel to the fire that burned inside the intense 6-foot-2, 206-pound senior.

Clinkscales had moved to Springdale from nearby Farmington before his eighth-grade year, only then coming out for football. He had played when younger, but as one of the bigger kids on the field, his time had been spent on the offensive line — hardly a glamorous position.

As he filled out in junior high, Clinkscales spent time at both fullback and linebacker — even switching to wide receiver before his sophomore year. Moving him around was an attempt by the coaches to determine exactly where "Clink" might fit best on the varsity squad. He had the desire and work ethic to succeed, but his upright running and unorthodox running style — as well as questions about his speed — left the coaches unsure if he could play running back on the varsity level.

Those questions were answered during spring practice after his sophomore season. There the coaches "put him through the ringer," as Malzahn said, repeatedly giving him one carry after another — "probably to the point he didn't want to go back in.

"And then we made him carry it some more."

As a junior, Clink slowly established himself as the team's primary running threat — breaking out with an 18-carry, 104-yard performance against Fayetteville. He went on to lead the conference in rushing that year, but he continued to feel as though the coaches didn't trust him or his ability. Those feelings only intensified following the season when the individual honors, such as All-State and All-Conference, were announced — with Clinkscales nowhere to be found.

"Damian (Williams) didn't even play the whole year (missing several games with an ankle injury) and he's All-State?" he asked. "Man, whatever."

The anger burned inside him as he thought about what he perceived to be a slight by Malzahn, leaving him quietly to say, "Just wait til next year." It only increased during the spring as his more heralded teammates began receiving all of the recruiting attention.

In the summer, he, along with several other teammates, attended a football camp at the University of Arkansas under head coach Houston Nutt. He was furious the next day when he saw an article trumpeting the presence of the "Fab Five" at the camp, with no mention of him.

Clink was one of the more well-liked members of the Bulldogs, his eagerness to smile and friendly personality making him also a respected leader as his senior season began. His feelings of animosity, however, toward the attention being received by The Springdale Five were present just beneath the surface — causing outbursts such as the one against Van Buren.

He had been angry at Malzahn after receiving no carries in the game against Prescott, but to have the same thing happen again was too much for him as he stood on the sidelines against Van Buren.

Again, Malzahn wouldn't talk about the incident. Other coaches, however, quickly pointed out that both of the games Clink hadn't gotten a carry in were against the Bulldogs' two weakest opponents. Plus, each was followed by one of the stronger ones — Jenks after Prescott and the conference runner-up from the season before, Fort Smith Northside, following Van Buren.

"Why go out there and risk getting him hurt when we don't have to?" one said.

Clinkscales' due came in the following game against Fort Smith Northside. Led by another of the state's top quarterback prospects, junior Kodi Burns, the Grizzlies were the last regular-season opponent to stay within shouting distance of the Bulldogs.

The 2004 game had come in the next-to-last week of the regular season and the Bulldogs were unprepared for the elusiveness of Burns. Springdale eventually won, 35–17, after leading by four at halftime, and that memory fueled speculation that Northside might be the only conference foe that could give the Bulldogs a close game.

During the week prior to the contest, newspapers hyped the quarterback matchup.

Mustain's focus the week of Northside wasn't on Burns, no matter how many times he was asked about a potential rivalry with his counterpart. His focus, as well as that of many of his teammates, was on making amends for the close contest from the year before. If ever there was a time to send a message to the rest of the state that the Bulldogs would not be beaten, or even challenged, this was it.

It was a message delivered loud and clear — in the form of a 52–0 shellacking, a game which Springdale led 45–0 at halftime before pulling its starters. Clinkscales rushed just seven times for 63 yards, but he did score three touchdowns on short runs, soothing any hard feelings.

At Mayo Thompson Stadium in Fort Smith, the crowd filled the seats and surrounding areas. Many of the faces were the same as in weeks before, but others — some with no ties to either team — had begun following the Bulldogs from place to place. The attention and the pressure were growing with each and every week — as evidenced by the incidents with Norman and Clinkscales.

They were minor problems when compared to the bigger picture of the season, but it had been minor issues such as jealousy from a few older players and distrust which had caused problems the year before. The difference between that group and what the current crop of Springdale players were going through was that the team a year before had expected to win a state championship regardless of what happened off the field.

The 2005 Bulldogs, however, assumed nothing. They knew even the smallest problems could erupt and keep them from achieving their goal, so regardless of whatever personal animosity existed, "Come Friday night, there's not going to ever be a problem," Mustain said.

"I'm going to take care of my business and I know everyone else is going to do the same.

"We can't screw this thing up."

• • •

Brad Marveggio stood at midfield at Jarrell Williams Bulldog Stadium, watching as his son, Derek, walked toward him. Springdale was just minutes away from kickoff of its regular-season finale against Rogers, and on the verge of completing its second-consecutive perfect regular season, but the game couldn't start until all of the Bulldog seniors were honored in front of yet another overflow crowd.

Fans had already filled the stands and taken their places standing behind the white picket fence that lined the field as Derek made his way toward his dad. Derek dreaded the moment, because he knew his dad wouldn't be able to keep from crying.

"My dad, he's a nut," he said. "I got my mom's genes, and he's a wimp."

He loved his dad more than he could probably ever tell him face-to-face, but Derek believed in following his mother's advice.

"She didn't want us grieving," Derek said. "My mom was like 'That's something you better not do, stand around my grave and cry.'

"'You've got to pick up the pieces and go.'"

His time for reflection and memories was saved for his time alone in the woods. It wasn't that he bottled up his emotions; he simply let them out on his own terms — away from others.

Derek was right about one thing regarding his dad; he and Brad were nothing alike when it came to expressing their emotions. Throughout Derek's senior season, Brad had found himself crying often when he began to think of how proud he was of Derek — and how proud Bev would have been of her baby boy.

"She'd be proud of him, man, playing at Springdale and all," he said. "And you're dang right I'm proud of him."

As Brad and Derek approached each other on senior night, public address announcer Bill Carter — whose booming voice usually echoed throughout the stadium for pregame introductions and touchdowns — softly introduced Derek. He also introduced Brad and Trish — as well as "the late Beverly Marveggio."

The last sentence was all it took for the tears to begin flowing from Brad's eyes as he reached up and wrapped his arms around his son's neck for a hug. He was greeted with the typical embarrassment of a teenage son, but that didn't stop him from pulling Derek close. It was as if the last three-and-a-half years of mourning had done something Brad never could have imagined — they had turned his son into a man right before his eyes.

"I've faced (the adversity), and I just took it like I was supposed to," Derek said.

"It always gets darker before it gets lighter. It got dark for a few years, but now it's getting lighter."

CHAPTER 11
Second Thoughts

THE TENSION HAD BEEN BUILDING IN MITCH MUSTAIN FOR OVER TWO MONTHS, BUILDING WITH EVERY ARKANSAS LOSS. He watched several games from the sidelines as the passing woes that had plagued Houston Nutt's offense during four years with Matt Jones at quarterback continued with new signal caller Robert Johnson.

"We're doing more stuff on offense every week on a high school team than they are," Mustain said. "And they're in the SEC."

He was there as the Razorbacks lost at home to traditional SEC doormat Vanderbilt. Afterward, he returned home worried about his choice of colleges.

He watched the game against the University of Southern California on television the night after Springdale beat Jenks, Oklahoma, reacting in horror as the defending national champion pummeled Arkansas 70–17 before a national audience.

"They could've scored 100. It was like watching us beat up on somebody," he said, referring to Springdale.

He watched as the Razorbacks dropped to 2–6 with a loss to South Carolina, ensuring that they would fall short of the six wins needed for bowl eligibility. It would be the second straight losing season for the program, coming on the heels of six straight years of trips to bowl games under Nutt. It was before that game that Nutt decided to pull the redshirt off freshman Casey Dick and play him the final four games of the season, a decision which caused even more concern for Mustain.

Mitch had no intention of something similar happening to him. He wanted to redshirt his freshman season, spending time watching and learning the college game while also getting stronger in the weight room.

"I remember when I was a sophomore and got into a varsity game late in the season," he said. "Everything was just moving so fast that I was just trying not to get killed.

"It slowed down when I was a junior, but even that was fast compared to what it's been like this (his senior) year. I mean, I can sit back there now and see routes open up before I've even dropped back.

"It's like slow motion."

During the season, Mustain watched the "same-old boring offense" by the Razorbacks.

Under increasing pressure from fans for his conservative play-calling, Nutt stood firm against those who called for him to hire an offensive coordinator.

Mustain knew all too well what the fans wanted because he had been a fan — at least up until now when his future was hanging in the balance. Never particularly fond of Nutt, Mustain felt slighted that the Arkansas coach had only contacted him a few times since his commitment and not once in six weeks.

The lack of contact was not his only problem. He had heard of happenings on the Arkansas team and coaching staff which had him concerned about his future. First, there had been the USC thrashing and he had heard the rumors of coaches and players yelling at each other on the sidelines during the second half. Not just normal in-the-heat-of-battle yelling, but coaches and players cursing at each other. He had also heard the rumblings of a confrontation between first-year Arkansas defensive coordinator Reggie Herring and Fayetteville High coach Daryl Patton, a confrontation over the treatment of Herring's son, Adam, who was a junior at the school.

What finally sent him over the top were the constant Internet rumors about the future of the Arkansas coaching staff. For all of his concerns about Nutt, Mustain did get along well with quarterbacks coach Roy Wittke, who had been the main Arkansas coach to recruit him. He liked Wittke's laid-back personality as well as what he seemed to know about a passing offense.

The only problem was that it didn't appear as the season went along that Wittke was having much input on the Razorbacks offense, unlike what Mustain had been promised would happen during his recruitment. His role was to assist with the play-calling in the passing game, but Mustain had heard and read on message boards that offensive line coach Mike Markuson was overruling much of what Wittke was sending in.

Rumors about Wittke's future had been around since before the season. In the articles Beck Campbell was angered about the past spring Nutt had said that he hadn't known Gus Malzahn was interested when he hired Wittke. The talk — both of Wittke's future firing and Malzahn's hiring in some capacity — was a constant source of chatter on message boards and talk radio.

It was like a soap opera, an evolving sequence of events with no ending, all beginning with the same person.

Mustain questioned whether Nutt was in charge of his own program.

"Here's the thing," Mustain said. "When you look at Texas, who do you think is in control?

"It's (coach) Mack Brown.

"When you look at Miami, who's in control?

"It's (coach) Larry Coker.

"Notre Dame?

"Charlie Weis.

"So, when you look at Arkansas, you tell me who's in control …

"Is it Houston Nutt? No way.

"Is it (athletic director) Frank Broyles?

". . . Who knows?"

Mustain didn't know who or what to believe when it came to the future of the coaches. His guess was that Wittke wouldn't be around next season and Malzahn would be at Arkansas in some capacity. And at this point, with the Bulldogs about to begin preparing for the first round of the playoffs, he didn't care. He was tired of the gossip about Nutt and his coaches and the losing by the Razorbacks.

He wanted out of his commitment, which is what finally led him to pull aside Bartley Webb the week before Springdale's game against Rogers, the final regular season game of the year.

"Do you think Notre Dame might still take me?" he asked of his surprised teammate, who had committed to the Irish in July.

Webb gave Mustain the phone number for Irish coach Charlie Weis, whom he called later that day. What Weis told him surprised Mustain, who had expected a quick affirmative from the coach.

Instead, Weis told him that it was his policy not to talk with recruits who were already committed to another school, as Mustain was to Arkansas. However, Weis did dangle a pair of carrots for Mustain to chew on before the conversation ended. He said the school already had commitments from a pair of quarterbacks and he didn't know if there was room for a third. But, he added, one of the quarterbacks had told him during the summer while the Irish were recruiting Mustain that if the Springdale signal caller committed to Notre Dame, he would go somewhere else. Weis also told Mustain that if he were to withdraw his commitment from Arkansas after Springdale's season ended, he'd be happy to talk.

That was all Mustain needed to hear before coming up with a plan to do just that. As soon as the season ended on December 3 — after the Bulldogs had won the state championship, of course — Mustain would get ready to withdraw his commitment to Arkansas. He needed a trigger to use as his reason and the likely firing of Wittke would be the perfect excuse.

Mustain knew his plan meant being less than honest with those who thought his commitment to Arkansas was still solid. However, Malzahn had made it clear that no recruiting talk would be allowed during the season, and Mustain wasn't about to put the state championship at risk with his distractions.

Mustain's plan was sweet music to his mother's ears. Campbell hadn't liked or trusted Nutt since the moment Mustain's father showed up at a recruiting event against her wishes. She had kept quiet about Nutt during the final weeks of recruiting in the summer, but she could cut loose now that her son had changed his mind.

She didn't like the way Nutt buddied up to select members of the media who reported on recruiting in the state. She didn't like the way that every time either she or Mustain said something to one of them about the school, Nutt or one of his assistants would call shortly thereafter "just to see how everything's going." Such an instance occurred the week before, after one reporter heard of "something going on" at Springdale and began calling his friends to ask about Mustain's status. The following day, Nutt called Campbell for the first time in months.

"That's some pretty nice timing, isn't it?" Campbell asked. "You know (the reporter) went straight to (Nutt) and told him something was going on, but he didn't know what and that's why he called."

More than anything, Campbell didn't like Nutt's "rah-rah" personality, saying "his act has worn thin."

"He has done the worst job of recruiting of any of the coaches we have dealt with through this whole thing, and he's going to get what he deserves," she added. "We've barely heard from him, and nobody over there (at Arkansas) has called to let us know what is going on.

"I don't trust him for a second."

She was looking forward to the day when Mustain would tell Nutt he wasn't coming to the school. She knew it would be a shock to both the coach and the state, and it would bring to the public light just what a poor job of recruiting Nutt had done — with no contact or assurances to her son during the Razorbacks' difficult season.

"This state is in for a big surprise come December 5," Campbell said of the day Mustain would likely withdraw his commitment. "Because that's when all hell is going to break loose."

With his decision already made on how he would proceed after the season, Mustain sat down in front of the television on the Sunday night following Springdale's first-round playoff win over Jacksonville on Friday and Arkansas' win at Ole Miss on Saturday. It was only the third win of the season for the Razorbacks, and it was quarterback Casey Dick's second as a starter. The Arkansas quarterback had thrown for 175 yards in the win, though the Razorbacks still ran the ball 16 more times than they threw it.

Mustain heard that following the win, Nutt had commented about the pressure he was under concerning his play-calling, but the quarterback was unsure what the coach had said. As the 10 o'clock news turned to sports, Mitch's eyebrows lifted when a still picture of Nutt came on the screen. It was followed by a recording of the post-game interview on the statewide Razorback football radio network with host Chuck Barrett.

"You know, (Dick) got man-to-man coverage on that last touchdown," Barrett said. "Was that a called play? Did he check into that?"

"That was a called play, and I called it, Chuck," said Nutt emphatically, followed by extended laughter by both.

"All right; well, congratulations coach."

"Hey Chuck, and I made some good calls today, too, brother."

"You sure did, you sure did."

Immediately afterward, Mitch stood up from the couch, pointing at the television.

"Oh my God, did you hear that?" he said. "Old 'H' has lost it. He has absolutely lost it. How can they let him get away with that?

"They ought to fire him on the spot.

"Of course, they'd have a better chance of getting me if they did."

CHAPTER 12
On to the Playoffs

OUTSIDE HIS OFFICE, GUS MALZAHN STOOD ALONE IN THE ROOM NORMALLY OCCUPIED BY HIS ASSISTANTS. They were all gone now — off teaching classes on this Monday morning — leaving him alone to concentrate on the Bulldogs' upcoming first-round playoff game just four days away.

He was looking at the far wall, scanning the Springdale offensive play-calling tendencies assistant coach Chris Wood had written on the dry-erase board. He looked over the numbers before glancing to his left, eyeing the blocking schemes offensive line coach Don Struebing had drawn up for that week's game with Jacksonville.

Here, with only football on his mind, Malzahn enjoyed himself the most.

In his earlier days, the rush of competition drove Malzahn. It's what made him something of a high school legend in his hometown of Fort Smith and what prompted him to walk on as a receiver at the University of Arkansas. Even then, there was something else to Malzahn. Friends and family said he was "intense" and "wise for his age."

As he made the transition to coaching, the thrill still came on Friday nights, but it was preparation that drove him. Without putting in the work, there would be no rush, no wins. That was the lesson he learned in his first season as a head coach in Hughes, Arkansas. Malzahn started as a defensive coordinator in 1991, following a stint as a volunteer assistant at Henderson State University, the school he chose after realizing he "wasn't good enough to play at Arkansas."

Malzan finished with a 4–6 record that first season, his only losing season as a head coach. He felt terrible, both for himself and the players. It was enough to send him searching for answers.

He headed home to Fort Smith. There, at one of the town's high schools — Southside — head coach Barry Lunney had proven himself as one of the state's top high school coaches and was someone Malzahn respected. He sat down with Lunney that summer, asking questions from everything about coaching offense to developing a more detailed practice routine. It was then that he began to understand the personal sacrifice needed to win.

It was also then that his seemingly natural ability to lead began to be noticed by those at Hughes.

"He always had that confidence about him," said Hughes Athletic Director Charlie Patrick. "He was always sure of himself. Plus, he would listen to you, and I mean really listen.

"To me that was his biggest asset. Some leaders are so big-headed they just push you off, but not him."

Malzahn rebounded in his second year at the school, finishing 6–4, but it was that third year when his newfound work ethic and organization really paid off. The Blue Devils finished 10–4 that season, reaching the state championship game in the process.

During that season, Malzahn's time at work began to increase dramatically. Instead of spending time at home on the weekends with his young family, he was spending countless hours at the school — watching film and studying his next opponents. He would arrive at his office early Saturday after games on Friday night, leaving just long enough for an afternoon nap. On Sundays, following church, it was back to the office until late evening.

Whatever it took to find that one play or tendency which would make the difference the following week.

The season after the state championship game appearance, Hughes finished 8–3, its third-consecutive winning record. Afterward, Malzahn again talked with Lunney, this time about a job.

He was set to take a head coaching job at a junior high in Fort Smith when a call came from a tiny private school in Springdale, Shiloh Christian. The school was looking for a new head coach and Malzahn's winning ways and exciting office had drawn attention. Close to taking the job in Fort Smith, Malzahn instead chose Shiloh.

"It's interesting to think sometimes about what might have happened if some things had been different in life," Malzahn said. "I really wanted to work with coach Lunney, but then Shiloh popped up."

Shiloh was 6-6 in Malzahn's first year. But, using his no-huddle offense that included a passing attack unlike anything seen by most small schools in Northwest Arkansas, the Saints began 1997 with 14 consecutive wins. In the championship game for the first time, Shiloh lost to Barton, but with many players returning the following season, Malzahn realized a championship was in his grasp.

Such expectations put great stress on Malzahn. Shiloh earned its first state championship that year, posting a 15-0 record, but he had lost 30 pounds, down to 170 by the time it was over.

"He looked like a stick figure with glasses and big ears," said his wife, Kristi.

It was during that season that Kristi — who already did most everything at the house while Gus was away — began to retake some control of her husband's time. She had never complained about paying the bills or keeping their two teenage daughters (Kylie and Kenzie) most of the time, nor had she minded attending all of the games he coached. It was simply part of being a coach's wife and family, a fact she and her daughters accepted.

"We've accepted that this is his ministry and calling in life," Kristi said. "The girls have an ownership in what their dad is doing."

As Gus' time away on the weekends continued to increase, Kristi finally had enough. She started limiting him to four-hour stints away from the house between church services on Sundays and asking that he spend Saturday evenings at home. His health — and the health of their family — was too important, even though she knew Gus was likely never to change.

"I do worry that he's going to get so into a game and keel over at some point," Kristi said. "Probably while he's screaming at a referee."

Despite his time at work being limited on weekends, Malzahn found new ways at Springdale to keep his players focused on the upcoming game. He scheduled separate film-watching meetings after practice for certain positions and gave players DVDs early in the week to check out their matchups.

At Springdale, his weekend routine was similar to his days at Shiloh. The offensive coaches came together on both Saturday and Sunday in the large meeting room usually reserved for the entire team. Malzahn would sit at the front of the room, sipping on coffee while using the remote control to watch the upcoming team's defense.

The defensive coaches met on the opposite end of the upstairs portion of the fieldhouse, in the team's equipment room. There they watched the offenses of opposing teams, diagramming each of their formations while co-defensive coordinator Kevin Johnson stayed in the outer room for the most part — looking for tendencies while moving the film from videos to the office computer.

Some of Malzahn's assistants joked that if he took a college job, his biggest problem would be adapting to the NCAA limits on time spent with players. It was a joke that was told more often as the 2005 season began, because those same assistants were acutely aware of the rumors surrounding Malzahn's future. The comments by Arkansas head coach Houston Nutt in the spring about wanting to hire Malzahn two years prior had been one reason, as well as the constant rumors on message boards and talk radio. Everywhere they went, it seemed, someone wanted to know if Malzahn would be sticking around or leaving.

The coaches and players weren't the only ones hearing the rumors. Malzahn's daughters had also read about their dad's future on a Web site, www.getgusonthehill.com, dedicated to promoting Malzahn for the Razorback staff. The site including a clock counting down the time until the end of the Springdale season and offered T-shirts for sale with a picture of the coach on the front. Such speculation made Malzahn uneasy. He had said the year before that he was committed to staying at Springdale with the group of seniors that included the Springdale Five, with no mention of anything beyond that.

Malzahn never directly denied the possibility of a future at Arkansas. Instead, he steered the conversations back to Springdale's season. Such an approach halted most questions but nothing was off limits during the weekend film sessions with his assistant coaches.

Offensive line coach Don Struebing felt "honored" to coach with Malzahn, and deep down he also hoped that one day Malzahn would be able to bring him into the college game. Of the assistant coaches on the Springdale staff, Struebing was the one most likely to broach any subject with a joke or story of some kind. He was also the one to give Malzahn the most grief about his rumored future.

"Coach, I've just got to know," Struebing said to Malzahn one Saturday in the darkened film room. "Which side of the 'A' are you going to run out next year?"

He was alluding to a pregame ritual at Arkansas, one in which the band forms a large 'A' on the field and the coaches and players run through on the way to the sidelines.

"Are you going to follow Houston down the right side or are you going to go your own way down the left?"

Also, on the morning following Springdale's opening-round playoff win over Jacksonville, he had another caveat for the coach. In the 44–8 win the night before, junior kicker Alex Tejada — another player expected to receive extensive recruiting attention the following season — had kicked a school-record 55-yard field goal in the second quarter. Tejada had excited the Springdale crowd at other times during the season — such as when he sent a kickoff 70 yards through the uprights against Rogers — but his field goal against the Red Devils brought them to their feet for an ovation.

"I've never seen so many people stand for an attempted field goal in my life," Struebing said the next morning. "It's kind of like when coach Nutt calls a play down the field."

His comment was in reference to the sarcastic applause that had begun at Razorback games recently after Arkansas had called a pass play. Mustain hadn't been the only one noticing the discontent with Nutt by Arkansas fans, and the comment drew immediate laughter from the other coaches in the room who knew Struebing was trying to elicit a reaction from Malzahn. He had no luck, as the coach continued to watch film.

"Come on coach, you know you want to laugh," Struebing said.

"I smiled," Malzahn said, not turning his head from the film he was watching.

Up next after Jacksonville was Benton, a senior-laden team out of central Arkansas. Springdale had last played the Panthers in the first round of the 2003 playoffs and that season was the last where Malzahn felt he still had players from the Jarrell Williams era. It showed in the 41–0 victory, a game in which Springdale's Zach Butler rushed for 240 yards. That team was hardly a prototypical Malzahn team, unlike the one that awaited the Panthers two years later.

The morning was filled with the usual watching of film by the offensive and defensive coaches. Malzahn did make a point to mention he had thought "all along" that Benton and West Memphis — the defending state runner-up — would be the teams Springdale would have to beat on its way to a championship. Other than that, the coaches didn't see any reason to worry based on what they saw. The Panthers had underachieved for much of the year, finishing second in their conference, and had struggled in a come-from-behind win the night before in their first-round matchup over neighboring rival Bryant.

The relaxed tone changed midway through the morning when Struebing received a call on his cell phone. On the other end was a friend who was the brother of a Benton player. The friend told Struebing that the Panthers coaches told their players after the Bryant win the night before that they had a special defensive plan in the works for Springdale, one which they hadn't used all season.

"He said they've known all year they'd have to go through us," Struebing said.

Struebing said the plan included double-teaming Damian Williams, single-covering Andrew Norman and sagging off junior receiver Zack Pianalto. He was also told the Benton coaches had studied film of Springdale for more than a week, completely overlooking and neglecting their game with Bryant — a team they had already played earlier in the season — in the process.

"So, they're going to single cover Norman?" Malzahn asked. "I like our chances."

The phone call piqued the interest of several of the assistant coaches. Offensive coordinator Chris Woods was particularly excited, not that he actually expected a game. He was simply looking for something to fire up himself and the players and he had found it.

"You know what this means, they've been scheming all year for us," Wood said. "That's fine . . . If they want to play chess, then we'll play chess.

"We'll unleash our monster (tight end Ben Cleveland, who had spent much of his senior season on defense)."

A few minutes later, Malzahn left the film room to make some of his own information-seeking phone calls about what Benton had planned. He returned a while later, saying one coaching friend told him that Benton coach Marc Jones was "telling everybody that it's his last year, so he's going to run it up on everybody.

"They think they're really good."

Springdale scored on its first possession for 7–0. On Benton's following possession, the Panthers drove to the Bulldogs' 2, where they had a first down. Quarterback Josh Langley tried a sneak, moving the ball a yard. Three more tries failed and the Springdale defensive players rushed off the field, knowing the tone had been set. Springdale led 42–0 at half on its way to 49–0. So much for a surprise.

"You know, the truth is we hear a lot of stuff like that," Malzahn said of Benton's alleged scheming. "Usually the game gets here and they always end up doing the same stuff, but it's still fun to make us think a little."

The next week, in the semifinals, the Bulldogs faced another team from central Arkansas, Little Rock Catholic. The Rockets entered the game riding an 11-game winning streak. The school was also riding a heap of momentum provided by head coach Ellis "Scooter" Register, a longtime high school coach in the state who had come to Catholic three years earlier, quickly turning the football team into a winner.

Springdale's coaches had little doubt that Catholic would be just another speed bump on the road to the championship game during the week leading up to the game. However, some of the players were keenly aware of a few similarities between this game and the loss to Little Rock Central a year before.

For starters, it had been in the semifinals where Springdale had lost to the Tigers. Add in the fact that Catholic and Central shared the same initials and you had reason for superstition.

One person who was anything but superstitious was co-defensive coordinator Kerry Winberry. The longtime assistant coach had other thoughts on his mind leading up to the game, primarily about a decision he had made several weeks before. He had decided to retire from coaching after the season, preferring to focus on just teaching for the rest of his career.

"It's just the right time," Winberry said. "What better way than to go out on top."

He felt the decision was the right one, but also one that brought with it a sense of finality leading up to his last game at home. Winberry hadn't told the other coaches he was leaving and he wasn't sure how he would handle his final walk off the field as a coach.

By the time the Bulldogs took the field that Friday night, one of the largest crowds ever to witness a game at Bulldog Stadium awaited. Some estimated that more than 10,000 packed the stands and other areas around the field. They were two-deep around the white fence that lined the field, as well as on the street outside the chain-link fence on the open north end. Just before kickoff, police officers had to usher a group of children off the red padding that stood in the back of one end zone. They were on the field looking for any possible place to sit, but none were left.

One group of friends in the stands had traveled from Memphis to watch the team they had read so much about. Looking ahead, they knew they wouldn't be able to attend the state championship game in Little Rock the following week, so they jumped in their car that afternoon and made the nearly five-hour drive to Springdale. They came to see Springdale, the future of the Razorbacks — not knowing of Mustain's internal doubts and future plans.

The superstitions some of the players thought about during the week were on their minds early in the third quarter. Catholic had scored a touchdown on the first possession of the half, closing the Springdale lead to 21–14. It was the closest any team had been to Springdale in the second half of any game that season and the feisty and physical Rockets were not intimidated.

Springdale ran the ball down the field on its following drive to take a 28–14 lead, and then the floodgates finally opened. The Bulldogs held Catholic on its next two possessions, and after each stop it took just one play for Springdale to score. The first touchdown came on a short pass by Mustain to Williams, who sprinted 60 yards for a touchdown and the next came on a deep pass to Andrew Norman, who was uncovered.

The quick barrage stretched the Springdale lead from seven points to 28 in a matter of four minutes, ending any realistic hope for Catholic and securing the Bulldogs' trip to Little Rock with the eventual 49–14 win.

"We did the best we could," Register said afterward. "We kept it close for a while, but we got beat by a great, great football team."

As the crowd continued to file out of the stadium afterward, the team's seniors gathered with Malzahn near midfield for a team picture. Winberry stood off to the side, looking at the visitors' stands which had been full just a while earlier and then back at the home stands in front of which he had spent so many Friday nights during his 33-year career.

"That was it," he thought. "That's the last time I'll ever coach in Bulldog Stadium."

"What a way to go out."

CHAPTER 13

Road to the Rock

JUST AFTER 7:15 A.M. the day following the win over Little Rock Catholic, Gus Malzahn sat outside his office with a few early-arriving assistant coaches.

The night before, the Bulldogs had punched their ticket to "The Rock" and a state championship date with West Memphis the following Saturday night. The Blue Devils had lost in the past two championship games to Little Rock Central and were also undefeated through thirteen games in 2005. They were also the team Malzahn had quietly expected to face at War Memorial Stadium throughout the season.

Malzahn and his coaches took a few minutes that morning to read over the morning newspapers, checking scores from playoff games and sharing what fellow coaches had to say about their games.

Chris Wood wasn't speaking to anyone in particular when he reminded them just how good the team was he had left during the spring, proudly pointing out Nashville's win over Highland in the quarterfinals the night before.

"I've got some ownership there, you know," Wood said. "This was too good an opportunity, and I had to leave, but a part of me is with those kids."

After about 15 minutes of relaxed conversation, one coach came across the West Memphis story in his newspaper. The Blue Devils had defeated the Bulldogs' fellow AAAAA-West Conference foe, Fort Smith Northside, in overtime to advance to the championship game. It was a game that Northside appeared to have won late in the fourth quarter until the Grizzlies inexplicably left a West Memphis receiver uncovered on fourth-and-long, resulting in a game-tying touchdown. The game marked the second consecutive year the Blue Devils had defeated Northside in overtime in the semifinals.

"Wow, they had it won it looks like," Dennis DeBusk said, leaning back in his chair at his desk.

"When's Hartsfield coming?" Malzahn asked seconds later, referring to the longtime Springdale Central Junior High coach who had traveled to West Memphis the night before to scout.

Two minutes later the conversations were over and the offensive coaches followed Malzahn into the film room, preparing to break down the Blue Devils.

West Memphis coach Lanny Dauksch had a style all too familiar to Malzahn. He had come to the Blue Devils from McGehee, where he led the school to the 1999 Class AAA state championship. Prior to that, Dauksch had been an assistant to legendary coach, Frank McClellan, at Barton High School in eastern Arkansas. McClellan was famous in the state for his eight small-school state championships over his career and was the state's all-time winningest coach with an overall record of 367–75–4. His name was also known in national high school football coaching circles, thanks to a state-record 63-game winning streak in the mid-1980s.

In December of 1997, Malzahn made his first championship game appearance with Shiloh Christian. The Saints' opponent that chilly afternoon at War Memorial Stadium had been McClellan's Barton Bears. Using his power running attack, McClellan frustrated Malzahn and Shiloh for much of the game, keeping the ball on offense and punishing the Saints on defense as the Bears took a 54–30 win. The same blueprint was what the Springdale coaches expected from Dauksch.

As Malzahn sat in his chair just a few feet from the projection screen, preparing to start the film of the West Memphis-Fayetteville game in the quarterfinals, both Wood and Don Struebing were already behind him discussing what they knew about Dauksch.

Wood had attended a clinic given by the West Memphis coach a few years back and was trying to remember where he put his notes. Struebing also remembered a seminar given by Dauksch, one with a fitting title, given the championship-game matchup.

"It was called, 'No huddle, no problem,'" Struebing said just loud enough for Malzahn to hear.

The offensive coaches began by isolating individuals on the Blue Devils' defense, noting their strengths and weaknesses. However, much of the discussion was about what Dauksch would do on offense, with Malzahn letting the film roll while the Blue Devils were on offense rather than fast-forwarding to defense as was usually the case during the coaches' Saturday morning meetings.

"It doesn't really matter what we do; the game is going to be won over there," Rhett Lashlee said, pointing to the door on the other side of the room. "We've got to stop the run."

One of Woods' questions was whether West Memphis would play a stall game, using up the play clock and running the ball as often as possible, just as Fort Smith Southside had done earlier in the year.

"Oh, you bet he is," Malzahn said. "He'll go for it on fourth down from anywhere."

"Yeah, if he gets fourth-and-two, that's what he wants," Wood followed.

After the film of the Fayetteville game ended, the coaches took a brief break, with Malzahn crossing the room to check on the defensive coaches while offensive assistants stayed behind.

As Malzahn left, Wood's thoughts strayed from the moment.

"You know what you need to get out there this week," he said. "You need to let all the Arkansas fans know that if they really want them, if they really want them to flip, then they need to come out and let them know it on Saturday (at the championship game).

"They need to show up, calling the Hogs, and make a statement about where they want these kids to go."

Wood was referring to Damian Williams and Ben Cleveland and their commitments to Florida, and with rumors beginning to circulate around Springdale High about Mustain possibly wavering on his commitment to the Razorbacks, his timing was suspiciously perfect.

Just after 9 a.m., the offensive coaches took a break from discussing Dauksch's work ethic and spotted Hartsfield, who had slept in following his five-hour drive from West Memphis.

"They announced 21–14 Springdale over Little Rock Catholic in the third quarter last night over the loudspeaker," Hartsfield said.

"I bet they liked that," Malzahn said, grinning.

Hartsfield spent 30 minutes filling in Malzahn on the basics of Dauksch's game. Tidbits such as "When they come, they don't hide it" on defense and "On offense, they'll hammer and hammer you until they find something" were about what was expected.

The Blue Devils' offense was run-based, primarily from a wing-T formation, using misdirection and quick-hitting plays to look for big gains behind senior running backs Marquette Williams and Xavier Murry. Against Northside, the powerful Murry had done most of the running with Williams battling an ankle sprain, but the Springdale coaches fully expected the speedy senior to be ready for Little Rock.

The formations, both on offense and defense, were nearly identical to what Malzahn had seen against Barton in 1997, although West Memphis' offense was more predicated on the big play than Barton's had been.

"This group breaks the big run and scores quickly," Malzahn said. "That's better for us if they score quickly because it gives us the ball back."

After more game film, Struebing and Wood continued to discuss their experiences with Dauksch, with Struebing saying the West Memphis coach had asked for diagrams of Springdale's blocking schemes after his seminar.

"Did you give them to him?" Wood asked.

"No way," Struebing quickly said.

"Good," Wood followed even more quickly.

As Hartsfield prepared to leave the office, Malzahn told him about the size of the crowd at the Catholic game. The junior high coach looked up at Malzahn through his thick glasses and said, It really seems like the end of an era; only one more Springdale football game."

"You know, it hit me last night," Malzahn said, though his monotone voice didn't show any extra emotion. "But what a way to go out."

Meanwhile all the discussion of Dauksch and his ties to Barton and McClellan made DeBusk wonder.

"You know what, I'll bet McClellan is sitting in Lanny's office right now helping him," DeBusk said.

"All those guys in the east stick together," Malzahn said, recalling his days at Hughes and how his fellow competitors in the east had ostracized him after he left for Shiloh.

DeBusk quickly stood up and left the film room momentarily, coming back in with his cell phone to his ear. His call was to McClellan's cell phone, and his chin jutted out with a sly smile when the Barton coach answered.

"Frank, it's Dennis DeBusk," he said. "You're not over there helping Lanny, are you?"

Turns out McClellan had been at the West Memphis-Northside game the night before and he had watched some Springdale game film afterward with Dauksch. McClellan told DeBusk he didn't think there was any way for the Blue Devils to beat the Bulldogs, but just fact that he was in West Memphis told the Springdale coaches he held out a slight bit of hope otherwise.

The call relaxed the coaches for a moment.

Meanwhile, Malzahn sat in the front of the room, the wired remote to the VCR in his right hand and a cup of coffee in his left. After the latest tape finished rewinding, he headed to his office, closing the door to make a few calls to friends – all coaches, of course — to see what they thought of the matchup. When DeBusk poked his head in a few moments later, he found Malzahn leaning back in his chair, hands resting on his head. Malzahn had turned his attention to the national rankings. The Bulldogs had climbed as high as No. 2 in one poll, but they weren't likely to move up unless others failed.

He quietly asked DeBusk what more the coaches could do to "push" Springdale to the national pollsters.

"I'll tell you what, if we win this thing, even if it's not by the mercy rule, we've still got to be one of the best in the country," Malzahn said. "I'd sure like to play Southlake Carroll because I'd put this group up against anybody.

"It sure would be nice to get No. 1, even if it's in just one poll."

• • •

Alex Tejada wandered throughout the fieldhouse just after 7:30 a.m. the Friday before the championship game. The buses, a charter for the seniors and starters and a garden-variety yellow school bus for the rest of the team, had not yet arrived, as the time to depart for Little Rock neared.

Tejada hated the cold, and what greeted him that morning was cold unlike most early December mornings. Not only was the chill enough to cause frost and ice over most car windshields, it had combined with a stiff wind that cut through even the thickest of black warmup pants worn by many of the Bulldog players.

On this morning, however, the cold was the least of Tejada's concerns. As he rummaged both through his locker and the coaches offices upstairs half awake, the normally light-hearted and jovial kicker turned sour at the realization that he couldn't find his jersey.

While waiting on the bus, Derek Marveggio joined his teammates inside the fieldhouse in the foyer, dressed in his football sweatshirt and wrapped by a layer of camouflage overalls, camouflage gloves and a camouflage hat.

"This isn't cold. Now, the deer woods, that's cold," he said, followed by a series of grunts and chuckles from his surrounding teammates. "Heck, this ain't even early compared to what I normally do on the weekends."

"Typical Marveggio," one deep and weary voice rose from the crowd.

As the buses wound their way around the parking lot and through the parked cars before finally stopping in front of the fieldhouse, assistant coach David McGinnis leaned over the upstairs railing to ask if anyone had seen Tejada's jersey.

"Way to go, Alex," one teammate remarked for all to hear.

On the charter bus there was a rush for the seats in the back by some of the lesser-known seniors, though none tried to take the single two-seat row in the very back. Those seats were for massive offensive lineman Bartley Webb and his claim to the territory was respected by his teammates, more so because of Webb's every-man personality than the intimidation his size could afford him if he wished.

As Webb shifted to get comfortable, with his headphones plugged into his digital music player and wrapped around his neck, the bus continued to fill up. Russ Greenlee and Aaron Finch sat together directly in front of him on the left side, with Andrew Norman a few rows up to the right and Mitch Mustain in an aisle seat on the left side.

Hunter Collyar, the reserve running back who had marked his seat before going back into the fieldhouse, returned a few minutes later to see special teams ace Corey Stewart in his spot a row behind Norman. Collyar leaned over Stewart and told him to get up; Stewart reacted by standing and shoving Collyar across the aisle.

"Don't put that one in the book," Webb joked.

Every seat in the Bulldog gym was taken for the pregame pep rally that morning, with the players entering after the short ride from the fieldhouse parking lot. As Webb walked through the double set of glass doors and into the building, he noticed that teachers, administrators, parents, media members and others stood in every nook and cranny. Ahead of him, Malzahn stopped briefly to shake hands with well-wishers before heading to the gym floor. He stood alone, waiting to speak, intermittently adjusting his watch, pulling up his pants at the thigh and fidgeting with his shirt.

He was ready to get on the road and he was ready to go now. It was his lead the players followed after the pep rally ended, grabbing bags of snacks that parents had ready for them on the way back to the buses. Webb, frosty air showing as he took a breath, quickly snared his bag before making his way down the aisle and to his spot in the back.

"That's the way to travel," he said.

The buses were led by a Springdale police escort down Pleasant Street before turning right on Sunset and heading west. Thirty minutes after the buses had pulled onto I-540 heading south through the mountains, Malzahn sat at the front of the bus reading the newspaper.

Earlier in the week he called his coaches into a closed meeting to address rumors of his departure to the University of Arkansas. Malzahn didn't confirm that he had been contacted by the college, but he promised they would be "the first" to know if something happened.

His future was also on the minds of his Springdale players as they made their way to Little Rock. As Malzahn turned the page in the sports section, Greenlee looked up, his eyes trained on his head coach.

"He's gone, right?" he said, partly asking while also making a statement. "I mean, look at him sitting there. You know he's as good as gone."

"We all know the answer to that," Webb answered.

• • •

Dinner on the Friday prior to the championship game was at a pair of restaurants near the hotel. Backup defensive lineman Brandon Windam sparked uncontrollable laugher from his teammates when he abruptly stood up and darted outside, throwing up twice for no apparent reason.

As several of the players stood to leave, a businessman, dressed in sport coat and tie and sitting with his wife, stopped them with, "You guys are from Springdale, right?"

After an acknowledgement, and with his wife's eyes open wide in awe of the players, the man followed up with, "Good luck tomorrow night, but I don't think you'll need it."

Malzahn gave his players a choice — stay at the hotel after dinner or to go a playoff game 10 minutes away. There was no doubt about his preference. "The more I can keep them around football and thinking about football, the better," he said.

The game between Ashdown and Central Arkansas Christian was under way when the charter bus from Springdale motored across the bridge over I-430 and up the hill into the parking lot at the CAC campus in North Little Rock.

He had called the private school to ask that a spot be reserved for his team and CAC responded by setting up temporary bleachers on the corner of the southwest side of the track that surrounds the football field. The request was a good thing, given the late arrival and the capacity crowd.

As they wound their way down the hill from the parking lot, Springdale's players did so in relative anonymity despite Cleveland's letter jacket with the red Superman "S" on it. The crowd's attention was on the Class AAA semifinal between defending state champion CAC and Ashdown, the team that had ousted Shiloh Christian a week earlier.

Mustain stood on the second row of bleachers in the middle of his teammates for much of the first quarter, with Webb a row below him and Malzahn a few rows above them, focused on the game. The quarterback received a call from Houston Nutt while he was there, with the Arkansas coach wishing him good luck the following day. He also saw Nutt's brother, Danny, the Razorbacks' running backs coach, on the CAC sideline with former Arkansas receiver Anthony Lucas.

However, his thoughts weren't on Nutt or the Razorbacks. Rather, they were on a phone call he expected to receive from Notre Dame on Sunday, the day following the championship game. It was during that call that Mustain expected to receive his scholarship offer from the Irish, although the plans were to wait until the week before the February 1 signing day to announce his commitment. That would give the Notre Dame coaches time to solidify that they had a spot open for him and to tell the two quarterbacks they already had committed that Mustain was coming.

"I am so ready to get going," he said. "I mean, we're talking about Charlie Weis and Notre Dame!"

As the first quarter wound down, Cleveland and Damian Williams grew tired of watching the game and left the bleachers to talk to some girls near the chain-link fence surrounding the track. Shortly thereafter, both Mustain and Webb followed to join the crowd which had gathered around the Springdale standouts.

On the way, Webb joked about Cleveland's easy-going personality and his ability to get along with anyone. Webb was greeted by three people wearing purple and gold letter jackets of Little Rock Catholic. One of them was starting linebacker Seth Armhurst, who wasted little time in shaking Webb's hand and complimenting the Bulldogs.

"You guys really are all that," he said. "We played West Memphis last year; the way you guys throw deep all the time, you'll kill them."

Twenty feet away, at the double gate which led from the area surrounding the track to the field, a pair of Little Rock police officers began to turn their attention away from the game and to the gathering crowd in the southwest corner of the stadium. One officer looked confused until his co-worker said to him, "That's Springdale."

Mustain grew bored with the conversation by the fence as the game approached halftime, so he and Cleveland left the track and headed up the hill and into the area behind the home stands to mingle some more. Just seconds after beginning the walk, a group of young children came running over to Mustain, all with borrowed pens and paper in hand, looking for an autograph from the icon they had heard so much about.

"Oh my God, you're famous," one said while handing his pen to Mustain. "I can't believe it's you."

Waiting his turn with hands at his sides, another one looked directly into Mustain's eyes and asked, "Do you remember me?" Mustain looked confused. "From War Memorial," the youngster said, referring to the Arkansas game Mustain had attended in Little Rock earlier in the season. At the time, hundreds of youngsters crossed his path, but he responded, "Oh, sure. How are you?"

Around them, however, not all of the crowd was as eager to give their Springdale guests a warm reception. One 30-something in a CAC hat made it a point to throw his shoulder into Cleveland as they passed each other, causing the gentle giant to think about retaliating before thinking otherwise.

As Mustain signed autographs, one fan in his early twenties began a running conversation. Mustain didn't hear the first question as he signed the forearm of a young CAC fan and he barely noticed the second one while signing the hat of a fan from Greenwood, one of the teams in the AAAA championship the next day.

Finally, he heard what the man was asking.

"You want to play in the NFL?" he asked, staring directly at Mustain.

"Hopefully one day," Mustain replied while continuing to sign.

"Well, you're acting like you're already there now," the man quickly responded, not looking away.

Mustain didn't respond, his right hand busy signing while his left clinched the hat he was holding in anger.

"If I had been anywhere else, I would have kicked that guy's ass," Mustain later said. "I mean, what did I do to him? I didn't ask for any of this, but here's this little redneck telling me how I'm acting?

"If I had been anywhere else, and I was anyone else, I would have pounded him."

• • •

Beck Campbell sat in the waiting room of a Little Rock hospital, biding her time while waiting for junior defensive lineman Jake Duron to have what looked like a spider bite on his leg checked. She didn't pay close attention to the television in the lobby until she heard a report on a local newscast that said Arkansas quarterbacks coach Roy Wittke had been fired.

She was furious. Neither she nor Mustain had been told about the firing of the one coach her son felt close to, but it was the timing of the report that had her upset. She knew Mitch was sure to hear the news that night, and it was the last thing he needed on the eve of the championship game.

Mustain had heard the news, but he was less concerned about it than his mother. To him, Wittke's firing was simply his prediction come true.

"It's going down just like I knew it would," he said.

The firing was the trigger he needed to bolt for Notre Dame, but that was for another day. Right now all that mattered was getting to bed tonight and West Memphis tomorrow.

CHAPTER 14
The Grand Stage

STANDING 5-FOOT-10 AND WEIGHING JUST 186 POUNDS, CHASE DAVIS DIDN'T INTIMIDATE ANYONE STANDING ACROSS THE LINE FROM HIM ON MOST FRIDAY NIGHTS. That is, until they looked into his eyes.

Chase Davis had grown up in Springdale and he knew what Gus Malzahn could do. When he was younger, he had seen the coach work his magic at Shiloh Christian when he coached Chase's older brother, Matt, a receiver for the Saints. And once his parents had given him the choice of high schools to attend before his freshman year, Chase made the move to Springdale High, although Malzahn and football weren't the primary reasons. They were just extra benefits.

Davis never had the size of most linebackers, especially those in the middle trying to stop the opponent's running attack. In fact, he weighed nearly 50 pounds less than the two players ahead of him on the depth chart before his junior year, which is why he worked so hard to prove himself.

What he had more than any other player on the team was toughness. He knew it, his teammates knew it and the coaches quickly discovered it during the spring practice of his sophomore year. He was never shy about throwing his body around to make a play.

The desire to be physical caused him to be scolded several times by officials during 7-on-7 action that summer in Alabama. Downing a player by just touching him went against his grain. The following fall, it was that mindset that caused him to shove a player from behind after the whistle during the first-round playoff game with Jacksonville. He knew better, but he was driven to retaliate against the player who had delivered the first blow.

The shove had led to a near melee at midfield of Bulldog Stadium. The officials, with the help of Springdale assistant coach Don Struebing — who rushed into the fray, throwing players back toward the sideline with one arm — quickly stopped any escalation. Malzahn had plenty of running waiting on Davis the following Monday as punishment, but the truth was he was just happy his starting linebacker hadn't been ejected from the game, a penalty that carried with it an automatic suspension from the following contest.

"He knows better," Malzahn said of Davis. "He just can't turn his engine off once it gets going.

"But it's what makes him the player he is."

Away from football, Davis was as laid-back and relaxed as anyone on the team, the son of a respected veterinarian and a normal high school kid who would just as soon spend an afternoon fishing as he would talking football. But he changed when it was time for contact. By game time, those who knew him knew better than to expect much of a conversation. He was as close to a real-life Dr. Jekyll and Mr. Hyde as possible.

It was a transformation that was necessary. He needed the rage, the scowl, the look to be able to throw his body into players heavier, stronger and faster.

That mindset was causing Davis anxiety on the morning of the state championship game. Kickoff was still more than nine hours away, but Gus Malzahn had gathered his defensive players in the parking lot of the team's luxury hotel in west Little Rock for an early morning workout. The intention was to keep the players on as normal a schedule as possible and to go over their defensive game plan one more time.

Davis had slept lightly, and as he stepped into the surprisingly warm morning air, he was thinking only of West Memphis. For him, going through the workout was as painful as playing 7-on-7. He was ready to hit, not talk.

Later that morning, as the players filed into War Memorial Stadium for the Class AAAA championship game scheduled for noon, Davis still could hardly speak to anyone, not even his dad who had called on the cell phone on the bus ride there.

Conversations would have to wait.

This game was for him. It was for his teammates. It was about avenging the Little Rock Central loss of the year before.

Defensive playbook in his arms, he walked through the tunnel to the seats reserved for Springdale players and coaches in the north end zone. Anytime he felt restless, he reviewed the plays he knew by heart.

For him, the playbook was a barrier against anyone who wanted to talk about anything other than the game.

It was chilly for the walk-through at War Memorial on Friday, but it was warmer this day with the early-afternoon sun beating down. Davis couldn't bear to watch football while the biggest game of his life was still almost six hours away and he walked down near the front of the section, seeking asylum. He laid down on the dirty concrete in the two feet of shadow from the railing above, resting his forehead on his folded arms, his playbook still in his hands.

All that mattered to him was that the game start as soon as possible.

• • •

The Springdale players began getting ready in the visitors' locker room under the southeast corner of War Memorial Stadium.

Matt Clinkscales sat quietly at one end, listening to music through his headphones. Another scholarship offer recently had come through from Arkansas State University, a Division I school in northeastern Arkansas.

Clinkscales was 75 yards away from 1,000, a number Malzahn and the other coaches had talked about throughout the week. Both the running back and his coaches intended for him to reach that magic number, a salve for being overlooked by major colleges and his failure to make All-State and All-Conference teams last season.

Malzahn was busy trolling for conversation from one end of the room to the other as the game approached. First he stopped by Clinkscales' locker to rehash what they had planned for the game's first offensive play. Then he walked over to Damian Williams and did the same. At one point, when he couldn't find anyone in his immediate vicinity to talk to, Malzahn looked down at his watch. It was just after 5 p.m., with less than 15 minutes until the special teams players would head to the field to begin warming up.

Springdale Central Junior High coach Fred Hartsfield stopped in for a moment to shake hands with two of his former players, Clinkscales and senior backup offensive lineman Kevin Flores. Mitch Mustain looked relaxed as he gazed around the room. He had his uniform on, ready to go, but most of his time during the final moments before game time was spent in casual conversation with those around him, not about the game. The only indication at all that he knew just what was about to happen was the fact he was chewing on what was left of his fingernails.

At 5:03 p.m., senior fullback Victor Pongonis, who had been sitting alone by a chalkboard on the west wall, stood up and called for everyone's attention. The sounds of the growing crowd could be heard through the open locker room door and the voice of the public address announcer bounced off the walls. But Pongonis had a few things to say.

"Pongo," as he was called by players and coaches, was as respected as anyone on the team. It was respect he had earned through his selfless play over the past two seasons, foregoing individual goals in favor of leading the way for Clinkscales' runs and a host of receivers who had followed his blocks en route to the end zone. He had gladly become the "2" in the "1-2 punch," the nickname he and Clinkscales had given to themselves before the season, one which they had put in white letters on the backs of their practice shorts.

Like many on the team, Pongo was a Springdale lifer. His older sister was All-State as a basketball player at Springdale before leaving to play college ball at Tulsa. He had grown up playing football and baseball with many of his teammates and had always been one of the quietest of the bunch.

On this night, though, Pongo wanted to share a year's worth of feelings and frustrations and he had written them as a poem.

He pulled out the piece of paper and, without looking up, began to read:

Here, a dream that was crushed from our minds
A year ago, there are still pieces we find
A game erased from our memory
When we lost to Little Rock Central you see
That game that crushed our perfect season
The game that crushed our dreams

We walked off that field with our pride hurt
Knowing that was the end
We couldn't go back, we couldn't redo
But we could try to rebuild and renew

Through offseason and spring ball
We couldn't get rid of a memory that haunted us all
We were determined to fight and become the greatest
To work like no other, we would work the latest

Denial not an option, we went to team camp
Where we came together and became a champ
A team when we left was what we had formed.

But now the media started to swarm
Spotlighting us like no other, we couldn't buy in
To what they would say to our mothers
We wouldn't forget, how bad it had felt, when 2004 came to a melt

Through airports and buses, we went all over the nation
Just to get stranded from our destination
Made fun of us for our helmets in big CA
We showed Cali the South football way

To 'Bama we went to show school pride
And came in second in top 25
It was finally here — two-a-days
When the game really starts to pay
Payoff for the work, as the season begins
To start off the games and win, win, win

We went through the conference hardly touched
But I am reminded of a kind of team of such
It was great but it was over
A new beginning was starting to lower

Time to start what really mattered
The games that brought the most chatter
We got to the game (where) we had lost so much pride,
and it was scary

For it had the same attributes as LRC I can't lie
In a hard fought battle we rose to the top
Here it was a chance to go pop

All I have is this quick thing to say
Don't forget to keep your emotions at bay
We made it, so let's not slip
This was our dream, we're going to the ship

But it's not over, don't wake up yet
For, we've got to finish strong
As a team united, here's our chance to live, our chance to shine
Give it your all, and leave it between the lines

It was the first time all season Pongo had spoken to the entire team before a game. His message, born out of the devastating loss to Little Rock Central a season before and the frantic year since, was simple.

Don't screw this up now.

"Think we can win," he said. "But know we can be beat."

• • •

Offensive line coach Don Struebing was standing in the south end zone, finishing a few friendly pregame conversations when the Blue Devils began filtering out of the northwest corner and onto the field. He drifted out as far as the 5-yard line as the players walked up and down the field, laughing and singing loudly along the way. They seemed relaxed for a team that had lost in the championship game the last two years, and Struebing tried to intimidate with a stare.

Previously, the largest crowd to witness a state championship football game in Arkansas was 15,207 in 2000. The record for any high school game was the more than 22,000 who had watched Springdale and intra-city rival Shiloh Christian at Razorback Stadium in Fayetteville in 2001. Malzahn had been a part of that game, but he was not prepared for the mass of people he saw when he looked up after exiting the tunnel that led onto the field. Springdale fans, the diehards and the casual ones, nearly filled the east side of the stadium. The west side was nearly full as well, with West Memphis faithful congregated close to each other in the middle sections and more casual fans surrounding them.

The relaxed attitude of West Memphis disappeared quickly. The Blue Devils won the coin toss and coach Lanny Dauksch chose to defer, exactly what Malzahn wanted. Springdale had scored on its first possession in each of its 13 games and the Bulldogs needed just two plays to extend that streak. Damian Williams accounted for all 65 yards, first by running 13 and then by taking a short pass from Mustain and winding his way through the defense for a 7–0 lead just 23 seconds into the game.

On the ensuing kickoff, Alex Tejada didn't get his full leg behind the kick and it fell to Marquette Williams just in front of the end zone.

The Blue Devils' leading rusher and best player tried to pick it off the turf, but he was hit and the ball went backward. Springdale sophomore Josh Fohner, convinced by Malzahn to stay one year at Springdale High before transferring to Har-Ber High, fell on the ball for a touchdown and 14–0.

The deficit began to take its toll on a deflated West Memphis, which managed only two yards on its next possession. Williams stuck another dagger in the heart of the Blue Devils when he ran 54 yards on the first play following a West Memphis punt. Less than three minutes into the game, it was 21–0.

The lead stretched to 28–0 late in the first quarter when Matt Clinkscales ran 13 yards untouched, and to 34–0 when Mustain found Andrew Norman down the right sideline for 59 yards with 3:37 left in the second quarter.

Despite the early onslaught, nerves, and turnovers, West Memphis didn't fold. The Blue Devils scored near the end of the first half, cutting the lead to 34–8.

The official attendance for the evening was 25,386. Although a large crowd had been expected, only a few gates were open and thousands missed the opening quarter while stuck in lines to get into the stadium. By the time the second half began, late-arriving fans from both sides of the stadium had spilled over into the north end zone. One long-time observer of games at the stadium disputed the attendance, estimating that the number topped 35,000.

West Memphis battled valiantly in the second half, even reducing the lead to 41–20 in the third quarter. However, the Blue Devils' running attack was too time-consuming for a serious comeback, and stopping the Bulldogs seemed unlikely.

The only surprise was that the Bulldogs had not reached the 35-point mercy-rule margin for the 14th straight game. They had their chances but, of all things, Tejada had bounced a pair of extra-point attempts off the uprights, a surprise considering he had made all 66 of his PATs as a junior.

Springdale had a chance to reach the 35-point margin late in the game after Pongonis' 10-yard run made it 53–20. However, Malzahn wasn't about to feed the notion of some critics that he was all about humiliating opponents, so he had Tejada kick with 4:05 remaining, a kick that capped the 54–30 final and the last scoring drive of the year.

Afterward, Dauksch — dealing with his first loss of the season — sounded like many of the other coaches the Bulldogs had handled throughout the season.

"I'm tickled to death," Dauksch said. "We knew what they could do and they did it. They just have so many weapons."

"I just wish we hadn't spotted them 21 (in the first three minutes of the game) and maybe the fans would have had a better game."

Bartley Webb was so excited about getting his hands on the Arkansas-shaped state championship trophy in the celebration following the end of the game, he did so before Malzahn could gather the team for the postgame speech. While Webb had wandered off with the trophy to the sideline near the Springdale student section, Malzahn brought the Bulldogs into a circle for the final time.

The dream had been accomplished, the expectations had been fulfilled. For their final act together on the football field, the 2005 Springdale Bulldogs confirmed for the entire state what most already knew. They were simply the best Arkansas had ever seen. They outscored their opponents 664–118 in 14 games, including an average of 35–4 in the first half when the starters were in — and they did it against both the best from Arkansas and elsewhere.

Damian Williams was named the game's Most Valuable Player for his 221 yards of combined receiving and rushing. His four touchdowns brought his season total to 36 in 14 games, or one for every third time he touched the football.

Mitch Mustain set a career-high for passing yardage in a single game with 344 yards and five touchdowns, bringing his season total to 47 touchdowns and just six interceptions. He completed 190 of 270 (70.4 percent) of his passes.

Thanks to his six catches in the game, the same number as Williams, Andrew Norman finished tied with Williams for the team lead in receptions with 63, though Norman held onto the career mark for receptions with 132. Ben Cleveland caught just one pass for a loss of three yards, but he tied for a team-high in tackles with 16. Bartley Webb helped the offensive line as it once again did not allow a quarterback sack of Mustain, finishing the year allowing just two.

"And one of those was the fault of the quarterback (who held the ball too long) and the other a running back," Struebing added.

It was the perfect ending to the perfect season.

And it was time for Gus Malzahn to finally relax as he hugged both Chris Wood and Kevin Johnson — his former Shiloh Christian assistants — on their way to the middle of the field.

"Guys," Malzahn yelled to the Bulldogs who had gathered around him. "Great job, great year. I've got one question for you.

"What's football?"

"SPRINGDALE!"

• • •

Chase Davis walked from one hug to another, his face still marked by the scowl he had worn during the game as he recorded all or part of 14 tackles. He wanted to smile; he wanted to enjoy the moment like his teammates around him.

Every time he started to relax, every time someone congratulated him on the game, he couldn't help but revert to gameday mode, unable to smile. He was having trouble letting go of his alter-ego.

This was it. This was the last time he was going to walk on a football field as a player. He didn't have a college scholarship to look forward to like his more heralded teammates. In college, players with Davis' heart also run like the wind and outweigh him by 50 pounds or more, a fact he long since had known but was only now beginning to fully grasp.

He had never planned on a future in football. He knew his destiny likely lay elsewhere, possibly following in his father's footsteps as a veterinarian. It was something he had always been comfortable with; he had never even given it much of a second thought.

Until now.

Lights on one side of the stadium had been turned off, leaving those on the field to take pictures and remember the moment in an eerie half-light, a fitting end to a dream season.

Davis held his helmet in his hands, seemingly unable to let go when he was asked if he had thought at all that day about what a championship would mean for Springdale, a championship in the final season before Har-Ber High opened varsity play. He had, he said.

"It won't ever be the same," he said. "But we'll always have this."

While others stayed on the field, talking and celebrating, Chase Davis took a quick look around the stadium which had been so electric and so full of people just an hour earlier.

With his head down, he headed up the ramp and into the tunnel to the celebration taking place in the lockerroom.

• • •

A few feet away, one of the recruiting reporters who both Mustain and his mother, Beck Campbell, viewed as a "pawn" of Arkansas head coach Houston Nutt walked up to Campbell. She had worked her way onto the field by pleading with a young security guard, only to be met there by Otis Kirk of the *Arkansas Democrat-Gazette*. Kirk was someone Campbell hadn't liked since the beginning of the recruiting process, for she had heard stories that he talked about helping the Razorbacks land players — though she had never heard him do so. She didn't like it when something Nutt said to her would be repeated in one of the reporter's columns.

Campbell also knew the only way recruiting reporters stayed in business was by getting their information directly from coaches. It was a highway of information she knew could be closed if the reporter irritated Nutt or refused to help the school get into the living rooms of recruits.

"That's his bread-and-butter," she said of Kirk.

Despite the celebration taking place around him, the reporter wasted little time in asking Campbell about Mustain's future.

"So what's Mitch going to do," Kirk said. "Is he going to open (his recruitment) back up?"

Campbell couldn't believe in the middle of celebrating her son's state championship victory she was already being asked about something which wasn't yet public knowledge and had nothing to do with what had just taken place on the field. Tonight was for enjoying the moment, the accomplishment of a goal her son had worked an entire year for.

She turned and walked away.

CHAPTER 15
All Hell Breaks Loose

MONDAY, DECEMBER 5

Mitch Mustain sat in the driver's seat, not feeling nearly as nervous as he thought he might.

He had told Arkansas coach Houston Nutt to meet him here, at a grocery store about a mile away from Razorback Stadium, for had he been seen walking into the coaches' offices on campus before lunch on a Monday, less than 48 hours after Springdale's state championship win, questions would have been asked.

The last thing Mustain wanted to do at the moment was answer questions. The anticipation of the next few minutes had been building for what seemed to be an eternity — more than five weeks, actually — but his decision had long since been made, and he was about to tell Nutt of his decision to rescind his commitment.

He waited while Nutt pulled in the space next to his truck and he quickly got out and into the Arkansas coach's black SUV. After a quick greeting, Nutt asked, "What's up?"

"Coach, I'm not coming," Mustain said.

"Awwwww, no," Nutt replied. "Are you sure?"

Of course he was sure. However, if his mom hadn't taught him anything else over the years, she taught him not to "burn your bridges because you never know how things might work out." During the conversation, Mitch focused on the uncertainty on the coaching staff. Nutt followed by asking several times what impact the reported firing of quarterbacks coach Roy Wittke had on Mitch's decision, but rather than use the firing as a false front, Mitch evaded the question.

The meeting didn't last more than 15 minutes, with Nutt asking Mitch not to publicly eliminate the Razorbacks. His concern at the moment was for the recruits still considering Arkansas, and the longer he could hide that he had lost the top quarterback in the country from his own backyard, the better, he told Mitch.

Mustain also had a request of Nutt as they parted ways. He didn't want the withdrawal of his commitment to go public, preferring to go through the next few weeks and to the U.S. Army All-American game without the hassle he had experienced during the summer of his initial recruitment. Besides, he knew where he was going, so why bother with all the attention again?

• • •

The first phone call came to the house less than two hours after Mitch had told Nutt of his decision. It came from a reporter from the statewide newspaper, the *Arkansas Democrat-Gazette*. It was the same newspaper at which recruiting writer Otis Kirk worked, though it was a reporter named Chris Bahn who was on the phone.

Bahn had worked hard over the past year to earn the trust of both Campbell and Mustain, with his initial "in" coming from his previous job, covering Springdale High football — when Mitch was a sophomore — for the regional newspaper, *The Morning News of Northwest Arkansas*.

However, Bahn's new beat was working with another conference school to the north, Rogers. In fact, the only significant time Bahn had spent around Mustain and the Bulldogs in the past year had been during the previous summer when he wrote a series of articles about The Springdale Five and Mitch's hectic recruitment. He had also followed Springdale to Little Rock for the state championship, writing a documentary on the team's final two days together.

Although she had let Bahn into her house during the summer for the articles on Mitch's recruitment, Campbell was wary of his phone call early that afternoon. First, she had worked furiously that morning at the Springdale fieldhouse with assistant coach Dennis DeBusk in determining all of the team's records, both school and state, and she was just plain tired. Added to that was the surprise party that night for Mitch when he would find out he had been named the Gatorade National Football Player of the Year in front of his family, coaches and teammates. Campbell knew the award was the first of three of the major national player of the year honors Mitch would win over the next month, but she wasn't about to let her son know and spoil the surprises.

The biggest reason for Campbell's wariness of Bahn's phone call, however, was his timing. Despite the fact she had privately shared some minor issues about Mitch's recruitment with Bahn in the past, she knew that morning's events were no minor issues and anything she said to him was likely to be shared with Kirk. She also knew that Kirk was unlikely to try to call either her or Mitch at this point, given all the negative things she had said to more than one person about both Nutt and Kirk. At that point in the afternoon, she didn't know what, if anything, Kirk had found out from Nutt, so she thought it was better not to say anything at all.

Bahn's initial inquiry, however, had nothing to do with Arkansas or Nutt. Rather, he asked about former Ole Miss coach David Cutcliffe, who had recently been rehired as offensive coordinator at Tennessee, the same job he had held when National Football League superstar Peyton Manning had been with the Volunteers. Cutcliffe had also coached the top pro draft pick in 2004, Peyton's younger brother, Eli, while at Ole Miss, and Bahn's question to Campbell related to whether or not his hiring at Tennessee would have any impact on Mitch.

Understand one thing about Beck Campbell: She is no Gus Malzahn. Whereas Malzahn has the ability to separate the person from the position they hold, Campbell is at heart a people person. She loves to talk to people, and the only way she knows to cope with her frustrations in life is to talk about them, regardless of the interest of the person she is talking with.

So as her conversation with Bahn began, she did something she had often done in the past. She assumed once the conversation turned to Nutt and Mitch that they had gone off the record, like before.

She should have known better.

It was a conversation she would later regret.

• • •

After spending much of his morning dealing privately with the fallout from his conversation with Mustain the night before, Gus Malzahn tried to get his day back to normal after lunch.

He was already reportedly in negotiations to leave Springdale and join the Arkansas coaching staff, fulfilling the long-rumored prophecy, but those negotiations had taken a back seat Sunday evening when Mustain had told him of his decision to withdraw his commitment to Arkansas and go to Notre Dame. Malzahn was shocked by the news, but he wouldn't admit it publicly for fear of the thought that he didn't have complete control of his program and knowledge of what his players were thinking, especially his quarterback.

Mitch knew Malzahn was already talking to Arkansas when he told him on Sunday, but even he was shocked to hear his coach express doubt, telling him, "How can I go if I can't even bring my own quarterback?"

"I understood his reaction though," Mitch said. "We hadn't talked about it in so long, since August, and I think he was under the impression that things were the same as in August."

The meeting had ended with little resolved, but the following morning Malzahn called with a plan, a plan that included Mitch telling Nutt of his decision as soon as possible.

Malzahn had spent most of the morning helping to set up the meeting between Mitch and Nutt, leaving behind the chaos at his office as Campbell and DeBusk worked on updating the record books. Now, as he settled in to his chair, he was about to enjoy the fruits of his first state title in six years by meeting with the players to pick out championship rings when his phone rang.

On the other end was a Central Arkansas promoter, a promoter calling with a question for Malzahn. Would the coach and his talented bunch of state champions be interested in playing one more game, a game against another of the top nationally ranked high school teams in the country, Lakeland, Florida?

The details were still sketchy, involving Springdale and Lakeland meeting on Saturday, December 17 — less than two weeks away — at the site the Bulldogs had just drawn more than an estimated 35,000, War Memorial Stadium in Little Rock. Lakeland was ranked No. 1 nationally by *USA Today*, while the Bulldogs were No. 4. In another poll by *Student Sports* magazine, Lakeland was No. 3 and Springdale No. 2. The only team ahead of the Bulldogs in both polls was Southlake Carroll in Texas, but that school's playoffs still had two games remaining. Lakeland, on the other hand, was set to play its state championship game in four days against Fort Lauderdale's St. Thomas Aquinas High and would be open the following week for such a matchup. The promoter said he hadn't contacted Lakeland yet; he was just gauging the interest level at Springdale first.

Malzahn knew deep down that the Bulldogs were tired, both mentally and physically. He had pushed them like no other group, and while they had always responded over the past year, he wasn't sure how quickly they could regain their fire after such an emotional season.

And there was the little matter of his future employment.

He put all the questions aside when he walked out of his office and into the room with the other coaches. His competitive juices were already flowing when he told the others about the phone call, asking if they would be interested in coaching in such a game.

"Heck yeah, let's go," offensive line coach Don Struebing said. "Bring 'em on."

The reaction was unanimous, although within minutes some of the coaches wondered aloud what such a game would do to Malzahn's expected, though not confirmed, departure from the school.

Within 15 minutes, the players found their way into the team's film room, where they had been so focused just a week ago. Now their attention was on everything but football, including Mustain, who sat in his usual spot on the front row, that morning's meeting with Nutt only known to him and a few others. The main focus of the meeting was to determine the look of the state championship rings, and after a few congratulatory remarks, Malzahn introduced a representative from a ring company.

Before the process for selecting the rings could be decided, however, Malzahn had one last thing he wanted to tell the team — there was a chance they could play again. A few voiced their support shortly after Malzahn told them of the possible opportunity, though most, including Andrew Norman, didn't believe Malzahn was telling the whole truth.

"No, I'm not kidding," Malzahn told them. "I just got the call."

During the discussion, Mustain sat quietly, thinking about the likely chaos if news of his decision got out. Like many of the others, he was worn out. The year-round work, the busy summer, and the stress of the season had taken its toll.

Senior linebacker Aaron Finch was the first to question whether or not to play. He had a ski trip planned the weekend of the proposed game, and more than most, he was just plain tired of all the attention.

"Oh, you'll play," Malzahn said, laughing off Finch, whose dulled expression didn't change. The coach then handed the meeting over to talk of the rings.

• • •

Beck Campbell walked down the staircase at James at the Mill, the restaurant just south of Springdale where her son's surprise party was about to be held.

Downstairs in the elegant restaurant, some offensive players, a group of Springdale coaches, and Gatorade representatives were waiting for Mitch. Looking around the room, Campbell was at peace. The place was calm and everything apparently was quiet on the "decommitment" front. Other than the phone call from Bahn about Cutcliffe and Tennesee, Kirk and Nutt had phoned, but she had been too busy to talk and quickly dismissed them.

The Gatorade-sponsored dinner was for those close to Mitch and the stairs to the room were monitored to keep out unexpected or unwanted guests. It was to be a night away from media or anyone who might have caught wind of the happenings that morning. A public event was planned at a pep rally for Mitch at Bulldog gymnasium the next afternoon.

Malzahn was at the point, in charge of pulling off the surprise. The Springdale coach had told the quarterback to wear a collared, button-up shirt and a nice pair of dress pants for a dinner with the mayor and other local leaders in celebration of the state championship, a completely believable story given the number of people at the championship game and the interest in the team at home.

Mitch was caught off guard when he walked in to see his teammates and coaches waiting.

• • •

Beck Campbell had warned before the regular season had ended that "come December 5, all hell would break loose." Little did she realize just how right she would be.

By the time he left the restaurant, Mustain knew that word of his decision was out. The calls were coming in fast and furious, and friends had told him that posters were discussing the possibility on the message boards.

Campbell soon learned that the talk going around was that her son had told Nutt he was reopening the process but keeping Arkansas on his list. The fact that Arkansas was an option at that point was untrue and she believed there was only one source of the information.

"That's coming directly from Houston Nutt," she said.

As for Mitch, rather than head directly home after the dinner, he instead made a stop at the home of Bartley Webb. The offensive lineman was meeting with Notre Dame offensive coordinator Michael Haywood, who had flown into Arkansas that day to meet with his recruit and future player. Mustain's appearance at the meeting was something that had come up as a possibility only after the quarterback had expressed renewed interest in the Irish to head coach Charlie Weis weeks earlier. After taking care of the decommitment from Arkansas, which Weis had set forth as a condition for re-recruitment, Mustain was more than happy to sit down and finally talk about his future with Haywood.

The three gathered around Webb's kitchen table that night, with much of the discussion focused on Springdale's state championship and Mustain's hectic day. Haywood told both Webb and Mustain that if the quarterback did decide he wanted to come to Notre Dame he was sure at least one of the two high school quarterbacks the Irish already had committed would switch to another school. He said one of the ways Weis would make sure of that happening would be by telling the recruits how intent the Irish were on offering one of the top juniors in the country the following year, California wunderkind Jimmy Clausen, and how his likely commitment to the school would hurt their future chances of playing. Of course, Haywood said, Weis wouldn't actually tell the recruits who he was talking about, so he wouldn't look bad when it was Mustain who took the spot of whomever withdrew their commitment first.

That's exactly what Mustain wanted to hear, but he was still concerned about whether the Irish coaches would be able to give him one of their 25 scholarships. He didn't mind the possibility of competing against either or both of the quarterback commitments, but he was not going to any school where he had to pay, especially one like Notre Dame, with an annual cost of about $45,000.

As excited as Mustain was about what he was hearing from Haywood, it was Webb who was even more thrilled at the chance his teammate and friend would join him at Notre Dame.

"It's going to happen," Webb said. "Haywood said they're going to drop one of the other guys to get Mitch, but they're going to do it in such a way that they don't look bad.

"It's going to happen, and I can't wait for (Mitch) to get the hell out of here with me."

The meeting came to a close well after 11 p.m. when Haywood, seated across from Mustain, had one final question for the quarterback.

"Can we count on you coming?" Haywood asked.

Mustain lowered his head, looking down at the kitchen table. Webb wasn't sure if his friend was having second thoughts about his decision, but the silence led him to believe so. However, after a moment, Mustain raised his head, with a smile spreading across his face.

"Yeah, coach, I'm coming," Mustain said.

He didn't get back home until after midnight on what had been the busiest day of his life, but when he did, Mustain wasted little time in checking out what was being written on the message boards.

His favorite was the one with the subject line: "Our worst fears are coming true."

It was after 1 a.m. before Mitch finally fell asleep.

"I'm so ready to get tomorrow over with," he said just before heading to bed.

• • •

Tuesday, December 6

Students filed into the wooden bleachers lining the basketball court inside Bulldog Gymnasium, while administrators and other adults found their way to temporary seats set up on the floor.

The assembly was the public version of the previous night's events at the Gatorade award dinner for Mitch Mustain. The bevy of television cameramen and reporters, who lined the wall behind the podium, didn't care nearly as much about the award as they did Mustain's plans. They had awakened that morning to a headline that his future was "in limbo" — a phrase used by Campbell in the article underneath. The piece was co-written by Kirk and Bahn, and since Campbell hadn't spoken at any length to Kirk that day, she knew the source of the quote. She had said it during her phone conversation with Bahn, but she though she was off the record after his questions about Tennessee and Cutcliffe.

Now she was regretting having talked at all.

[*Editor's note:* An article by the author also appeared that morning in *The Morning News*, stating that Mustain had withdrawn his commitment in a meeting with Nutt. Mustain told the author weeks earlier of his pending decommitment for the purposes of this book, and the article was only written the night before, after it became clear word had leaked out.]

Malzahn knew the questions would come quickly and from all sides about Mitch's reopening of his recruitment that morning. What he and Campbell didn't want, however, was for the award ceremony to turn into another recruiting circus. That's why they asked Springdale assistant coach Dennis DeBusk to serve in his public relations capacity that morning.

DeBusk's job was to inform every media member who entered the gymnasium that no recruiting questions would be allowed of Mitch, that the focus of the event was to be on the award. He told them that anyone who asked about recruiting would be quickly asked to leave.

The ceremony, which featured a number of city and state politicians all eager to capitalize on a photo opportunity with the state's golden-armed golden child, went off well, with only one hiccup. While presenting Mustain a certificate from the state Senate honoring his achievements, state Senator Jim Holt, a Republican from Springdale, told a story about the person who had written the certificate in Little Rock.

"She said, 'You let him know that if he decides to go anywhere else but to Arkansas to school and the Razorbacks, that we might have to reclaim this certificate,'" Holt said, a statement that was quickly followed by gasps and boos in the crowd. Obviously Holt hadn't read that morning's newspapers.

After the ceremony the media horde gathered around Mustain, though DeBusk stood just outside the circle, listening. He was still angered by the stunt one television reporter had pulled back in August when he had stepped in front of the camera before Andrew Norman could make his announcement following Mustain, and DeBusk was more than ready to give the reporter who disregarded his instructions that day "the boot."

Once they were done with Mustain, the group headed over to Malzahn. If Mustain wasn't going to talk recruiting they knew Malzahn wasn't about to say anything on the subject. Instead he focused on Mitch's achievements as well as informing everyone the proposed game with Lakeland, Florida, in Little Rock on December 17 wasn't going to happen.

It was a matter of logistics, he said, mentioning that the teams would have less than a week to prepare and that several of the Springdale players had already started basketball practice. Of course, he didn't mention the fact that his players were burned out and ready to get back to a normal life, nor did he talk about his own future, which was undecided at the moment after he had been contacted about possibly joining the Arkansas staff.

Oh, and his quarterback had other things to deal with at the moment.

CHAPTER 16
End of His Era

Gus Malzahn's hiring at Springdale High in 2001 made news across Northwest Arkansas as well as in the high school coaching ranks. His departure from the school, which had been rumored for months, was the lead story on television newscasts and in newspapers throughout the state.

Word of his hiring as the offensive coordinator at the University of Arkansas began to leak out on the evening of Thursday, December 8. By the time he met the following morning with the Springdale players, with stories already in that day's newspapers saying Malzahn had been offered the job, there was little suspense as to what he would say.

Pulled out of class just before 9 a.m., several players looked sullen as they headed for a meeting in the film room at the fieldhouse. They were only days removed from winning the state championship and their coach was about to leave.

The assistant coaches and school administrators who had gathered outside Malzahn's office were excited for their friend and for the Razorbacks, believing Malzahn would give the team a needed shot in the arm.

The coaches also had a sense for just how much respect Malzahn's hiring would bring to high school coaches across both the state and country. They also knew the impact it would have on the dreams of many young coaches because if Malzahn could make the jump from tiny Hughes, Arkansas, to the position of offensive coordinator at a Southeastern Conference college in less than 15 years, they could as well.

"I think it's great for the state of Arkansas and I think it's great for high school coaches all over the state," said Springdale defensive coordinator Kevin Johnson, Malzahn's rumored and likely successor as head coach. "It just brings a great spotlight on Arkansas and shows people that we play good football."

Malzahn walked toward the front of the room where he had given so many speeches over the past five seasons and calmly told the players that he regretted that the news of his departure had leaked out before he could tell them. He thanked them for their effort, promised he would watch them closely in the future and also asked that the underclassmen "stick together," alluding to the upcoming split between Springdale and Har-Ber Highs.

"It has totally been an honor to be your head football coach of the Bulldogs," Malzahn told the players. "We've reached the goal we set and you guys bought into the dream that we set and you've made it all come true.

"Those are some great memories, hopefully, you guys will have for the rest of your lives."

After Malzahn finished and stepped to the side, the players were silent. Prompted by the school principal, Allen Williams, they applauded, but even then it was half-hearted.

Williams promised the players a new coach would be named as quickly as possible but his reassurance did little to lighten the mood as the meeting closed. Malzahn stood at the back of the room, shaking hands and thanking his players as they filed out of the room and back to class. One, junior Eric Jones, who had come into his own on the field over the past season — finishing with 16 tackles in the championship game — couldn't even bring himself to look at Malzahn as he filed past and out the door.

Malzahn left Springdale with a 53–11 record over five seasons, 26–1 over the final two. He left with the state championship he had promised to himself and his players. He left riding a wave of momentum that was about to lead to calling plays at the state's flagship university.

Gus Malzahn left behind broken hearts as well.

• • •

Much like the rejoicing when Mitch Mustain and Andrew Norman committed to Arkansas in August, Gus Malzahn's move was celebrated by fans across the state.

It was a hiring those on the outside questioned.

Regardless of the debate surrounding his hiring, one thing was for sure when he walked into the media room inside the Broyles Complex just a few hours after telling his former players at Springdale that he was leaving. Gus Malzahn looked every bit the part of offensive coordinator at a Southeastern Conference school.

He sat just to the right of Arkansas coach Houston Nutt as the news conference began, dressed in a dark suit he had changed into since the meeting with his former players that morning. And though the announcement of his hiring was no surprise by the time the news conference began, the debate about his credibility was already being waged on message boards all over the Internet.

"How can they hire a high school coach?" one poster asked.

"The (Southeastern Conference) isn't exactly the AAAAA-West," another wrote.

Malzahn's jump to college wasn't the first for a high school coach, but his immediate ascension to coordinator in a top conference like the SEC raised eyebrows. Those with doubts included several national sportswriters who speculated that Arkansas hired Malzahn in an attempt to get Mustain.

Malzahn answered many of the same questions about his background at the news conference, as did Nutt, who said Malzahn's offensive mind was as good as any.

While Malzahn and Nutt spoke, members of Malzahn's family were in the media room. One leaned to his side while the questions about Malzahn's high school background continued.

"Can you hear that?" he asked. "Can you hear the doubters?"

The doubters he was referring to were those across the SEC who said the 40-year-old was in over his head. They were the same ones who said the Razorbacks were crazy to hire a high school coach and that Nutt would never really delegate his play calling.

It didn't matter what Malzahn's record had been in Arkansas or how well his offensive philosophy had worked for other coaches who had listened to him speak across the country. He always found a way to win, whether it was football, basketball, golf or softball.

"They can doubt him all they want," the family member said. "He loves that."

• • •

Mitch Mustain was angry and confused.

His coach and best friend, Gus Malzahn, had just accepted a job at Arkansas. He did it despite saying a few days earlier that he wouldn't take the job unless his quarterback was in tow. The day that Mustain backed out of his commitment, he made it clear to Malzahn that he had no intention of playing for Houston Nutt.

Campbell had told Malzahn to make his decision without considering Mustain's choice of schools. She wanted her son to make his decision based on where he felt he would be most comfortable. Right then, that was Notre Dame.

Mustain, Malzahn and their families were in New York together that week, and when the coach left the Big Apple earlier than planned, Mustain knew he was joining the Arkansas staff.

The group was in the city for a photo shoot with Mustain and former Dallas Cowboy great Emmitt Smith, the National Football League's all-time leading rusher. The photo session and interview were for a Parade magazine cover in January, which would name Mustain the national high school player of the year — his third such national award.

When they returned to Springdale that weekend, Mustain made it clear to his mother that Malzahn's hiring would not affect his decision to go to Notre Dame. He was adamant, seemingly angry with Malzahn for taking the Arkansas job. He even went so far as to tell his mother that he didn't want any of the Arkansas coaches, particularly Malzahn, making an in-home recruiting visit.

"I don't even want to see him," Mustain said. "I just want to get the next few weeks over with, sign with Notre Dame and get out of here."

Campbell wasn't sure how to react to her son's feelings. She understood the next few weeks would be some of the most difficult of her son's life — silently staying committed to Notre Dame while under assault at home in Arkansas — but at the same time, she wasn't about to let Mitch turn his back completely on the man who had been his friend for the past three years.

"What am I supposed to do?" she said. "Just tell this man who has been your coach for the past few years he can't come in?"

It was only during the days after their return from New York, when dealing with Mitch's hostility toward Malzahn, that Campbell began to understand what her son was feeling. In his mind, his friend had betrayed him. Those feelings were intensified by the pressure on Mitch and his closeness to Malzahn.

The roots of their friendship had begun when Mustain was a lowly sophomore, eager to make his mark on the varsity level, yet relegated for the most part to the sophomore team. Several of his sophomore teammates, including Andrew Norman, Damian Williams and Aaron Finch, became a part of the varsity team during that season, but no matter what Mustain did, he felt like it wasn't enough for Malzahn.

He thought Malzahn hated him and didn't respect him as a player. That's why, he thought, Malzahn had belittled him when he had come into a varsity meeting later in the season. Malzahn had told him to forego his sophomore team meeting that week in favor of the varsity one, but once Mustain had arrived, Malzahn stopped the meeting just long enough to ask, "What are you doing here?" and sent him back to the sophomores.

The incident, and the season, had left Mustain unsure of his future at Springdale for much of the winter and spring following his sophomore season. That is until he arrived for summer workouts that year. That summer of Mustain's breakout performance at Hoover, Alabama, there was a dramatic change in Malzahn's attitude toward Mustain, a calculated change.

To Mustain, this was a new Malzahn, somebody who could tell him how to play quarterback and advise him on life in general. It didn't matter if their discussions were about football or if Mitch had a problem dealing with his newfound fame. Malzahn was the one who was in the lead, steering his protégé through any potential pitfalls, always with an ear free and an eye on the future.

"He was just trying to make me better as a sophomore," Mustain said. "I thought he hated me, but that's what he wanted me to think so I would work even harder to prove myself.

"It worked out pretty well."

The tough love Mustain had experienced from Malzahn as a sophomore didn't completely go away during his junior season. In the Bentonville game that year he suspended Mustain for all but a handful of plays. Malzahn's reason was that Mustain had missed a practice during the week before the game, an unexcused absence. Mustain was on a school function that afternoon and he had told a teammate to tell Malzahn where he was, but the teammate either hadn't told Malzahn or the coach was simply trying to send a message about not pawning off responsibility on other people.

Either way, the suspension had rankled Campbell to her core, especially when Malzahn wouldn't say publicly following the game why he had suspended Mustain. It was her trust of Malzahn, however, which led her to stay quiet and not make a scene. She trusted the man to do what was best for her son.

In the days following Malzahn's hiring, Campbell began to understand the relationship between her son and his high school coach. They were so much alike that oftentimes they could be seen standing together in an identical pose, chewing on their fingernails.

Malzahn was not just a coach, he was the one male figure Mitch would listen to about life. But now, the relationship was in jeopardy. He was about to lose his father figure, his role model, his friend.

And Beck Campbell didn't know if her son would ever get that friend back.

CHAPTER 17
The Road to Home

RICK CLEVELAND COULDN'T BELIEVE WHAT HE WAS SEEING. He had just walked into the fieldhouse on the campus of Springdale High in the spring of 2004, and his eyes were wide open, his head turning from side to side as he looked at the framed player pictures in front of him.

To his left, a single door with a plaque above titled "Bulldog Country" led to a weight room like one he hadn't seen since his days as a football player himself at the University of Colorado in the early 1970s. Free weights dotted the room that spread out in front of him, a board listing the weight-lifting records at the school resting on the wall across from the entrance. In the corner, another door led to a training room, complete with examination tables and enough tape to bandage up the entire team.

On his right, after entering the fieldhouse another door led to the lockerroom. It was carpeted with wooden lockers lining the walls and jutting out in places to form a maze of helmets, shoulder pads and uniforms. Once again, the room reminded him of his college football days.

Nothing prepared Cleveland for what he saw as he exited the back door of the lockerroom and stepped onto the artificial surface. He quickly glanced up as he became aware of the size of the indoor practice field, a game-ready 50-yard surface, complete with yard lines and hash marks. With its high ceiling, the fieldhouse looked like a warehouse or a hangar big enough for a Boeing 737.

Rick Cleveland lived in his hometown of Arkansas City, Kansas, at the time, but he was in Springdale for a meeting with Gus Malzahn. Originally, he had been in the area to visit an aunt and look for potential places to move while doing odd jobs as a painter. During that visit, several people touted him on Malzahn and his program. That information touched a nerve because Cleveland was looking for a new opportunity for his son, Ben.

From the time he was born, Ben Cleveland was going to follow in his father's footsteps in athletics. The youngest of three children, Ben had grown steadily through middle school and junior high, even finding his way onto the varsity football team in Arkansas City as a freshman. However, a falling out with the high school coaching staff — over a perceived lack of playing time as a sophomore — had left Ben disillusioned with the game and more interested in basketball.

Rick Cleveland didn't mind his son's love of the game on the hard court, but after divorcing Ben's mother and struggling with single parenthood as Ben shuttled back and forth between his parents' homes, Rick had other ideas about Ben's future. Rick knew that while Ben — who had grown to 6-foot-4, 210 pounds in the time leading up to his junior season — had the size and soft hands to be a force on the football field, his size and position as an interior player on the basketball court likely wouldn't add up to a college basketball scholarship. That was the reason he had set up the meeting with Malzahn. He hadn't even talked to his son about the possibility of moving — and didn't know if the coach even needed a player like Ben — but he had heard too much about Springdale football not to at least look into it.

During their meeting on the second level of the fieldhouse, the indoor practice facility visible through the windows of Malzahn's office, Cleveland talked up his son's ability. He wanted to know if there were any starting positions open that would dovetail with his son's talent. And Malzahn said he could use a big receiver to complement a pair of talented juniors. The meeting ended with Rick agreeing to send Malzahn some video. Once Malzahn and Springdale basketball coach Charles Smith took a look, Malzahn called Rick and said, "Yeah, we can both use him."

The first time Ben visited Springdale, he wasn't sure about moving. However, a visit to the fieldhouse and Bulldog Stadium sold him, and he arrived in town for good just in time to join his new teammates for a camp at the University of Tulsa that June.

Ben's first season at Springdale High was curtailed by a broken collarbone suffered when a 300-pound lineman fell on him awkwardly during a game. Despite missing much of the second half of the season, he had impressed his coaches and opposing teams with his soft hands and agility. He returned from the injury the week before the loss to Little Rock Central, but didn't catch a pass in either of the final two games.

Although college coaches had film of Ben, recruitment of the tight end went slowly until the spring when coaches saw him in person. He had added 20 pounds of muscle and his stock soared. By the time the spring ended, Cleveland had surpassed several of his teammates in terms of recruiting attention with 10 scholarship offers, including Florida, Texas A&M, Iowa, and Arkansas. He was the fifth player from Springdale to be offered by the Razorbacks.

He committed to Florida during that summer following a whirlwind trip along the East Coast on the heels of the Alabama tournament. Ben was infatuated about possibly playing for new Gators' coach Urban Meyer, who had a reputation for throwing the football, much like Malzahn. He was so excited about going to Florida that he painted half of his room from floor to ceiling in the orange and blue of the Gators. The other half was painted in Springdale's maroon and white.

Some of his teammates weren't sure about Cleveland at first, but he ingratiated himself with his easy-going approach. Based on his drawn-out speech, they labeled him "dumb as a rock." The truth was he sometimes floated in and out of conversations because of attention deficit hyperactivity disorder. Eventually, he fit in because he was looking for laughs rather than serious conversation.

He had an ability to get along with everyone, especially with many of the children who sought his autograph as his fame grew. Ben was fascinated by their innocence and non-judgmental ways, with no more telling a moment than when he and other players visited Arkansas Children's Hospital in Little Rock the day before the championship game. There, while his teammates mingled and played games with a group of patients, Ben spent much of his time paying attention to a 2-year-old girl. The rules of the visit precluded Ben from asking what was wrong with the tiny brunette, but he didn't mind not knowing. The two played with dolls and other toys during the nearly hour-long visit.

"There's not a mean-spirited bone in his body," Rick said.

During the summer the coaches asked Ben to change positions. Rather than spending his time only at tight end, where he expected to play in college, Ben's big body was needed on defense, where the Bulldogs had been hit hard by graduation. Springdale had plenty of receiving options

(Damian Williams, Andrew Norman, a resurgent running back in Matt Clinkscales, and an up-and-coming junior tight end, Zack Pianalto). Malzahn told Cleveland he would still be used on offense, but he also wanted to see if he had the mean streak needed for defense.

The move paid off quickly for Ben, a factor at linebacker and defensive end from the first game on. The size, quickness and fearlessness that made him so adept on offense worked well on defense. Not only did he show the ability to pressure opposing quarterbacks, but he also surprised even himself by helping shut down opponents' running backs. In the state championship game, he tied with a team-high 16 tackles against the bruising West Memphis Blue Devils.

"There's not a lot Big Ben can't do," Malzahn said.

As soon as Malzahn was hired at Arkansas, Rick Cleveland knew the coach would call on behalf of the Razorbacks. Neither father nor son had any close ties to Arkansas, but both liked the school and the Razorbacks were in the running until the very end when Ben committed to Florida. On two fronts, Rick had reservations about sending his son down the road to play for the Razorbacks.

He was concerned about the lack of pass-catching opportunities for a tight end and he was unsure of Nutt's future.

"I didn't want to send my son to play for a coach that was going to be gone after one year," he said. "Then he'd have to start all over."

Arkansas' second consecutive losing season had created even more uncertainty about Nutt's future for Rick, who told Malzahn just that when the coach met with the Clevelands over the holidays. Rick said he was concerned about Malzahn's freedom to run the offense.

Malzahn's response was that he was in charge of offense and that the Razorbacks would play a similar style to what he had done at Springdale. As for Nutt's future, Malzahn only said, "Look, I'll be there for three years."

"What if (Nutt) is fired?," Rick asked.

"I can't promise you anything about that, but I can promise you that I'll be there for three years," Malzahn said.

"Coach, I believe that you believe what you're telling me," Rick said. "But, what I don't know about are the people who are telling you what you believe."

"Trust me, I'll be here for at least three years," Malzahn once again said. "I will not fail."

Ben switched his commitment from Florida to Arkansas just after the new year, with word leaking out while Mitch Mustain and Bartley Webb were in San Antonio for the U.S. Army All-American Bowl, featuring 78 of the top high school football players in the country. Ben's choice of Arkansas once again gave the Razorbacks two commitments from The Springdale Five, with Norman still on board.

Mustain knew of Ben's commitment before it was announced. The decision didn't come close to changing his mind about Notre Dame, but it again sent Arkansas fans into a frenzy of speculation.

For months, Beck Campbell had made it clear to her son and anyone else who would listen that she didn't trust Houston Nutt.

When Mitch told her of his intentions in November to go to Notre Dame, Campbell was almost relieved. Like her son, she had watched as the Razorbacks had continued to play conservatively on offense and the two of them shared doubts about whether Nutt would ever open up the offense, no matter who was the quarterback.

However, in the weeks following Mitch's decommitment from Arkansas, Campbell had become less and less sure of herself. She hadn't trusted much of what Nutt had said during the recruiting process, but as Mitch prepared to travel to the U.S. Army All-American All-Star game in San Antonio the first week in January, she was beginning to doubt the sincerity of all college coaches.

Notre Dame assistant Michael Haywood was the source of her latest doubt. On the night of his decommitment, Mustain promised Haywood he would play for the Irish if the school could find a scholarship opening. The coach responded that wouldn't be a problem. If needed, Notre Dame would hint to both of its quarterback commitments that they weren't likely to play since Mustain was coming, hoping one or the other would go somewhere else.

What had bothered Campbell since that time was that while Mitch had been ready and willing to express his commitment to Notre Dame publicly, Haywood continued to ask that he wait until the scholarship spot was for sure. Campbell brought the issue to Haywood's attention during several phone conversations, even going as far as to warn the coach that for every day he made her son wait, "the more of an opening you're giving coach Malzahn to come back in the fold."

As for Malzahn, during the week leading up to the All-American game, even though he had convinced Cleveland to switch his commitment from Florida to Arkansas, his work on Mustain was far from finished. He knew of Mustain's decision not to play for Nutt as well as how upset he was when Malzahn had left Springdale High for the Razorbacks. After passing a college coaching test that then allowed him to recruit players for Arkansas, Malzahn quickly made it a point to contact Campbell. He was looking for a way back into the ear of Mustain and he needed Campbell to show him the way.

"Be his friend, not a coach who's trying to recruit him," she told Malzahn. "Maybe that will work."

Mitch knew better than to think the speculation that had followed his every move over the Christmas and New Year's holidays would stop when he and teammate Bartley Webb left for San Antonio on New Year's Day. He just didn't realize how much awaited him during the week leading up to the U.S. Army All-American Bowl.

His decommitment to Arkansas had been national news over the past few weeks, with stories about the quarterback and his future appearing in newspapers and on Web sites from coast to coast. Whereas Malzahn had restricted the national media access to Mustain in Alabama the previous summer, no coach could have stopped the onslaught in San Antonio.

The All-American Bowl entered its sixth year as the self-described "single most important recruiting event of the season." The selling point was inside access to top recruits who were still undecided and the game was scripted so that those players could announce their decisions during the NBC telecast. Prior to kickoff, the media was given a schedule of the announcements and the game was often delayed while the announcements were carried on TV and shown on the large video screens inside the 65,000-seat Alamodome.

Organizers pressured the uncommitted players to announce their decisions and Mitch Mustain was on that list. Those in charge of the event salivated at the possibility that the top uncommitted quarterback in the country would share his choice with their audience. It was a bona fide meat market, Mustain thought, as he was asked repeatedly during the week if he was ready to make his decision.

He had traveled to the event a year earlier to watch several of his teammates go through an athletic combine for juniors who hoped to impress college coaches. With his arm still in a cast, Mustain wasn't able to participate. While posing for pictures with some of the other top junior quarterbacks in the country, he wondered about his future. Unable to even grip a football, he didn't know if he would ever play again.

Upon his return to San Antonio a year later, the doubts were about his college of choice. However, the constant pressure for a decision was making the week anything but fun.

One of the few relaxing moments for Mustain came on the night of the college football national championship game between Texas and the defending champion, the University of Southern California. Mustain had strongly considered playing for the Longhorns during the spring before a meeting at then-coach Gus Malzahn's house left him once again considering other schools. Mustain wondered aloud about what might have happened if he had chosen to play for the Longhorns. He knew his senior season wouldn't have gone as smoothly — not with the hatred that many Arkansas fans have for Texas from the days of the now defunct Southwest Conference — but he also wouldn't be in the position he was now, waiting on Notre Dame to find him a scholarship opening.

"If I didn't think they would have burnt my house down, I would have gone to Austin," he said.

During the Texas-USC game, Mustain paced back and forth in the room he shared with Bartley Webb. He was actively cheering for the Longhorns to win, which is what they did after a late touchdown run by quarterback Vince Young.

"That was awesome," Mustain said. "I was so pumped I couldn't stand it."

During practice, Mustain quickly asserted himself as the top quarterback on the West team. He was chosen to lead daily warm-ups and his accuracy and strong arm allowed him to distance himself from the other two quarterbacks. One of those was a Texas high school left-hander, Jevan Snead, who committed to the Longhorns and graduated high school a semester early to go through spring drills.

The daily practices were mostly individual drills by position. Such one-on-one battles provided coaches more instruction time and allowed recruiting reporters to gauge the accuracy of their talent ratings.

While Mustain was flourishing in the environment on the field, Bartley Webb was struggling both physically and mentally. During several one-on-one drills, Webb was thrown to the ground as defensive linemen rushed past him. He wasn't ready for the top-notch competition after having practiced only basketball for the past four weeks, and his early struggles compounded as the week progressed.

"This sucks so bad," he said. "I'm getting killed out there."

Webb wasn't the only offensive player struggling for the West. During a midweek scrimmage, the entire offensive line did little to stop the rush, leaving Mustain and the other quarterbacks exposed to big hits. Following the scrimmage, Mustain was frustrated at being continuously asked about his decision and the way the practice had gone. He was mad at what he perceived as a lack of intensity by several of the players, mainly the receivers. After watching his line struggle, he had a pretty good feel for Saturday's game.

"We're gonna get killed," he said. "I'm so ready to get this over with and go home."

Off the field, speculation regarding Mustain's decision increased during the week. Reporters watched his every move, reporting on his performance and his indecision about college. One report noted he was wearing a towel on his waist in Notre Dame colors inscribed "Play like a champion," the same phrase the Irish see in their lockerroom before games. The report prompted a series of posts on message boards, including one that said: "It's over. He's gone." The author contended Mustain was toying with fans without saying publicly he was headed to Notre Dame.

"The next thing you know, they're going to look at my belt or something," he said.

Mustain was doing anything but flaunting his decision. The towel was a gift from a family friend and he had put it to use following the state championship game. On the field after the rout of West Memphis, Mustain was approached by a young fan who asked if he could have the white towel hanging on his belt. Mustain had had the towel since he was a child, but the boy did the asking in such a nice way that the quarterback gave the towel away.

By the time the game arrived, Mustain's patience had worn thin. In addition to the speculation and frequent media attention, he was tired of organizers pressuring him to commit during the game. He had no intention of doing so — he had told them as much early in the week — but different people kept asking him and he finally hinted that he might, just to get them to leave him alone. During the pregame, his hint was teased by the TV announcers.

Mustain continued to worry about how the West would perform in the game. He even told Gus Malzahn, who had planned to travel to the game with Mustain before accepting his new job at Arkansas, about his worries.

"Well, just don't go out and look like an idiot on national television," Malzahn told him.

Unfortunately for Mustain, he did just that — with the game going just as he feared it might. While spending much of the game running from an oncoming rush, he completed only 2 of 13 passes for minus two yards. His only quality completion down the field came as he was leveled by East defensive lineman Robert Rose, an Ohio State commit, and it was called back because of a chop block penalty. Rose went around Webb on his way to Mustain, continuing Webb's week of struggles and drawing snickers from a few Internet recruiting reporters in the press box who had said before the game that Webb was "terrible and is going to get Mustain killed."

Making matters worse, on Mustain's only rushing attempt — a draw play to the right — he was in the process of sliding down when he had a helmet-to-helmet collison with Antwine Perez, who was headed to USC. The hit elicited "oohs" and "ahhs" and was shown on the replay boards. Mustain said the hit didn't hurt, but it did surprise him. That was evident to those closest to him who watched as he grabbed his facemask and pulled it down, just as he had done following the hit against Little Rock Central that had left him with a broken arm.

The West ran only 16 times and Webb said the emphasis on pass made it difficult for him and Mustain. Mustain's first nine plays were called passes. For the game, the coaches called pass plays on all but two of his snaps.

"Obviously, they knew we were going to pass," Webb said. "Everyone in the entire nation probably knew we were going to pass.

"(The East) definitely had their ears pinned back and were coming.

"I would have liked to have run the ball a little more, but we did have the best quarterback in the country and we wanted to showcase him."

• • •

A few hours after the game, Malzahn and his family went to dinner with Campbell, Mustain and his younger brother, Matt.

Mustain had received the news he had been waiting on for more than a month. A scholarship was open, Haywood said, and the school would take three quarterbacks if they all decided to keep their commitments. Mustain told Haywood that he would stick to his plan and travel to South Bend, Indiana, the weekend before signing day on February 1, to meet with head coach Charlie Weis and Haywood. After that meeting, Mustain planned to make his commitment public.

Aware of the development, Malzahn heeded Campbell's advice and limited any discussion of Notre Dame. Rather, the two families made their way down the famed River Walk, though the river had been drained for cleaning that week. Malzahn stayed at the back of the group, watching, knowing that if Mitch was going to change his mind, something would have to trigger the decision.

CHAPTER 18
48 Hours or Else

ITCH MUSTAIN'S CELL PHONE RANG ON THURSDAY, JANUARY 12, AND WHEN HE SAW THE NUMBER ON HIS CALLER IDENTIFICATION HE KNEW IT WAS NOTRE DAME OFFENSIVE COORDINATOR MICHAEL HAYWOOD ON THE OTHER END.

The Irish coach had told him a week earlier that a scholarship spot had become available. Both Mustain and his mother were relieved by the news, but she still doubted the sincerity of the Notre Dame coaching staff. She had not liked how Haywood had strung along Mustain over Christmas and New Year's and had told her son so.

Mustain, however, had not minded waiting. He had been told a spot would become available and he had taken Haywood at his word. It was that promise that had given Mustain the strength to tolerate the scrutiny and criticism he had received since the season ended.

His escape was his job at the local airport where he could sit in relative anonymity.

Mustain's plan, which he had discussed with Haywood, was simple. He had been ready to publicly commit to the school since December, but with the uncertainty about the scholarship spot he had understood Haywood asking him to wait.

The wait had given him time to think about how he wanted to make his departure from Arkansas official. Prior to his announcement, he wanted to visit the campus for a face-to-face with Haywood and Weis about the offense.

While in San Antonio, Mustain and Haywood had reviewed the quarterback's plan for a last-minute announcement and the coach was on board. For that reason, Mustain was surprised when he answered the phone on that Thursday and the coach sounded rushed and somewhat upset. He wasted little time in getting to the point.

Haywood said the timetable for Mustain's public decision had been moved up. He needed the quarterback to tell him for certain that he was indeed coming to Notre Dame because the school was about to offer California quarterback Jimmy Clausen, a high school junior, a scholarship for the next year's class. He said Weis also needed to know so that the coaches could tell both Zach Frazer and Demetrius Jones to give them a chance to leave if they wanted.

Haywood said the school was comfortable taking all three quarterbacks, including Mitch, in this class if they decided to stay, but the coaches were no longer fine with waiting until the weekend before signing day to tell them. That despite Haywood having agreed to Mitch's plan weeks earlier.

He gave Mitch two days to make his decision, but that didn't keep him from asking then.

"Coach, I can't," Mustain managed to say. "You're going to have to get back to me tomorrow."

Hanging up, Mustain was in shock. He had been pressured into making a decision before by schools, specifically Texas during the spring, but nothing like this. Here he was just over two weeks away from signing day and the plan he had thought was rock solid for more than two months was crumbling around him.

The coaches owed him a campus visit and a face-to-face after he waited five weeks for them to find him a spot, Mustain believed.

He wasn't sure what to do next. He had promised Malzahn he would make one more visit with the Arkansas staff the following week but that had been more out of courtesy to his former coach. Like his mother, he had warmed to the idea of staying with Malzahn in recent weeks, but every time he thought about it he would weigh the idea of playing for Houston Nutt versus Charlie Weis and come up with the same answer: Notre Dame. No matter how much he loved the Razorbacks or how much he looked up to Malzahn, he just couldn't shake the thought that he had heard all of the promises of changes in the offense before.

But, suddenly under pressure from Haywood, he put aside his concerns about Arkansas and called Nutt at 4:30 that afternoon.

"I was like, 'Damn, I've got eight hours to make a decision,'" Mustain said. "All of that time I thought I knew exactly what was going to happen, and then (Haywood) pulled that crap and he wanted a decision the next day.

"So I was like 'I've got eight hours,' and I was out of options. So if there was anything new I was going to hear from (Arkansas), it had to be that day."

When Nutt answered, Mitch asked if there was any way for the two to meet that day. Nutt said "Yeah, yeah," and asked if Mitch could meet at 7 p.m. at the coaches' office in the Broyles Center at Razorback Stadium. Relieved, Mitch agreed.

Five minutes later, his cell phone rang again. It was Nutt with bad news. In his excitement, he had forgotten that coaches were in a dead period under NCAA rules and couldn't meet with recruits.

Mitch's heart sank in that split second. All of his options were gone. Scholarships to schools across the country had been his for the taking and here he was.

"I was done," he said. "When coach Nutt said that, I was like, 'I'm screwed. I've screwed this up so bad.'"

His moment of fear turned a second later when Nutt asked, "Does your mom mind you being out late tonight?" Mustain thought the coach meant around 10 o'clock, but what he quickly found out was that he wanted to meet at one minute after midnight — a way to avoid breaking any NCAA recruiting rules since the dead period ended that day. Mitch felt like he didn't have a choice, and Campbell didn't mind either — as long as her son found a way to make a decision he was comfortable with.

When Mustain arrived on campus that night, awaiting him were all of the members of the Arkansas offensive coaching staff, including Nutt, Malzahn, offensive line coach Mike Markuson and new quarterbacks coach Alex Wood. The next morning, Mustain couldn't remember everything about his meeting the night before, but he was impressed that so many coaches had been there.

He didn't go to school on Friday. Campbell let him sleep in, calling to wake him around 8:30 a.m. Up and around but still weary from the night before, he called Malzahn to ask for another meeting with the Arkansas coaches and they decided on noon.

A while later, Haywood called again, once again asking if Mitch had an answer ready.

"Coach, I can't give you an answer," Mustain told him. "I had planned on taking a visit up there, and without that, I really can't give you a positive answer."

Haywood told Mustain that he needed an answer quickly so he could call Weis and give him the final verdict, but he agreed to give one more day.

"I'm going to call tomorrow and I've got to know," he said to Mitch.

At noon, Mustain again made his way to the Arkansas campus, where the coaches were once again waiting on him. This time he talked individually with coaches other than Malzahn. He and Wood talked for nearly an hour, drawing up plays on the dry-erase board that hung on the wall. Markuson came into the room, walking over to the same board while talking about Malzahn.

"I just want to let you know that people have been saying crap about me and Malzahn," Markuson told him before writing the names of his wife and children on the board. "Look, you're going to meet (Markuson's family) and I'm not going to screw this up. I've got a family to take care of."

Mitch left the meeting feeling comfortable for the first time since Haywood had put him on the spot the day before. He had had enough of the games, the pressure and the lying. He just wanted to play college football, and for the first time he was sure of where he wanted that to be — at home, at Arkansas.

"That's pretty much when I made up my mind," he said. "I was like, 'This is stupid.'"

Haywood did call him back the following day, that Saturday, but Mustain didn't answer. The coach and his boss, Weis, were just like every other college coach out there, Mustain thought, and they didn't deserve his final answer.

However, that didn't stop Weis from putting his spin on Mustain's decision. A few days after Haywood's call, an article by recruiting writer Mike Farrell appeared on rivals.com about Mustain and Notre Dame.

Farrell wrote of how forthright Weis had been over the past few weeks, claiming that when Mustain inquired about coming to the school during the regular season, Weis told him "No." Farrell wrote that Weis wasn't interested in Mustain because he had verbal commitments from Frazer and Jones and had promised he wouldn't take a third quarterback. He finished with, "Passing up on Mustain had to go against every fiber of (Weis') offensive coordinator being, but it was the right thing to do and Weis knows it."

Campbell's face turned redder than the blush on her cheeks when she read the article. She had been talking with Haywood for nearly two months in anticipation of her son playing for the "trustworthy" Notre Dame coaching staff, and she knew what she had read was false.

"They planted that crap with Mike Farrell just so they could look good for the national people," Campbell said. "Just so Charlie Weis could look like the good and honorable coach."

As upset as Campbell was, her anger didn't come close to matching that of Mustain's. When he called Nutt that following Monday to say he was indeed coming to Arkansas, he couldn't help but think about Notre Dame.

"So, I'm sitting here for two months, waiting for them to get a spot," he said. "And I'm getting my ass grilled. I mean, I'm getting hammered here for two months and I couldn't do a thing.

"And I sat around and waited for what, for this?"

He wasn't finished, not after re-reading the article by Farrell.

"Here's the thing," he said. "The thing was they hadn't officially offered me. But they always talked about getting me a spot, which they finally did while I was in San Antonio.

"They had a spot, and if I was going to tell them yes, then they were going to offer me. Basically, I was going to have to sign a blank contract.

"The thing that pisses me off is that I'd been getting hammered for two months here, two months while waiting on them to say it was OK to go public with my commitment," he continued. "I mean, I was getting raked on message boards and on the radio and I couldn't do anything about it.

"I'm sitting here waiting on them, ready to go, and then all of the sudden they come back with 'You've got 48 hours, you can't take a visit and we're going to offer Clausen and forget about you.'

"I got the shaft on that one."

His recommitment to Arkansas went public that night. At the time he wanted more than anything to get his rebuttal to Weis out in the newspaper but Malzahn said he shouldn't, preferring instead to focus on the positive of his future with the Razorbacks. Mustain agreed, but he couldn't let his anger totally go one last time after looking at the article on the computer in front of him.

"This crap makes me look like a liar and an idiot," he said. "Weis never talked to me; it was always Haywood. Now it's like I'm just this little beggar child saying 'Please take me.'

"Bullshit.

"I hope we play (Notre Dame) someday.

"I hope to God we do in a bowl game."

• • •

Beck Campbell sat in her living room as Mitch walked out the door. He left the house to start making phone calls to other Arkansas recruits, just like Malzahn had asked, leaving behind his mother to ponder the events of the past few days.

"Do you think his heart is really in this?" she asked. "Do you think this is what he really wants, or he's just so mad at Notre Dame that he felt like this was his only option?"

Over the past few weeks Campbell had made no secret to her son of her desire for him to stay at home and stay with Malzahn. She was contemplating her choice again when the phone rang. It was Houston Nutt on the line, calling to thank Campbell for allowing her son to come to Arkansas. Toward the end of the conversation, Nutt promised to "take care of" her son.

"You'd better," she said.

"Well, we'll find out if he made the right decision," Campbell said after hanging up. "We won't know for four or five years, but we'll find out."

• • •

Three days after Mitch Mustain's announcement was made public, Bartley Webb made his way into Bulldog Gymnasium for a basketball game that night.

He had decided to play basketball for the final semester of his senior season as a way to stay active in his preparation for college. However, after the first few weeks, his knees ached from running up and down the hardwood floors, his back hurt from the extra pounding and he wasn't happy about his lack of playing time.

It was that frustration combined with finding out that Mustain wasn't coming with him to Notre Dame that led Webb to unload his anger on his friend that night.

"He got cold feet, that's what he did," Webb said of Mustain. "He got nervous about leaving Arkansas and he got scared.

"He went from being a first-round pick (in the National Football League draft) to a third- or fourth-round pick at best. That is, unless he can run a 4.3 forty."

The last sentence referred to former Arkansas star Matt Jones, who had run the fastest 40-yard time in history for a quarterback at a professional scouting combine following his senior season. It was that time which helped vault Jones to being a first-round pick by Jacksonville, though his professional future was at wide receiver, not quarterback.

"But, that's OK," Webb continued. "He did what he had to do, and I'm going to do what I have to. I'm ready to get out of here, and I'm ready to start winning national championships."

CHAPTER 19
Signing Day

BARTLEY WEBB LAY AWAKE, EXHAUSTED AS THE EVENTS OF THE PAST SEVERAL MONTHS RAN THROUGH HIS HEAD OVER AND OVER, YET HE WAS TOO EXCITED TO FALL ASLEEP.

He had gone to bed at 11:30 p.m., but he watched the clock click toward 3 a.m.

In just over four hours he would sign his national letter of intent to play football at Notre Dame, and the enormity of that prospect was sinking in. The work, sweat and pain were about to pay off with a free college education. He would have a chance to play on national television every week for the school he had admired since watching the movie *Rudy*, the story of Rudy Ruettiger, a walk-on who had grown up loving Notre Dame.

It had been two weeks since Mitch Mustain had decided to say yes to Arkansas and no to Notre Dame. Bartley was no longer upset with Mustain, but he couldn't help think about what might have been.

"Why waste any time," he said. "I couldn't wait to get it over with."

After a quick bite to eat, he went to his dad's office and faxed the letter at 7:30 a.m. to the Notre Dame fax number listed on his instructions. He called another number a moment later to confirm receipt of the fax, and after being transferred to Notre Dame head coach Charlie Weis for a few congrats, it was official: Bartley Webb was going to be a member of the Notre Dame football team.

The same hectic build-up reached its conclusion for five other members of the 2005 Springdale state championship football team that morning. After all of the anxiety by Arkansas fans, four of The Springdale Five (Ben Cleveland, Andrew Norman, Damian Williams and Mustain) signed their letters with the Razorbacks and sent them to the school. Williams had become the final Bulldog to join the group at Arkansas, switching his commitment from Florida to the Razorbacks just a few days before signing day. Under intense scrutiny ever since

Mustain's decision, Williams stayed quiet about his plans, not even telling his parents until he was ready to announce.

The receipt of each of the players' signatures was reported on recruiting message boards, much to the rejoicing of the thousands of posters gathered online that morning.

Another player, running back Matt Clinkscales, also signed his full-ride scholarship that morning, but not with a Division I-A school. He had been offered by Arkansas State University, Arkansas' Division I stepbrother in Jonesboro in the northeastern part of the state. However, the school's location had outweighed its first appearance in a bowl game since 1970. Clinkscales instead elected to sign with the University of Central Arkansas in Conway. Former Chicago Bulls great Scottie Pippen played college basketball at the school, 30 minutes north of Little Rock. It was also the alma mater for some former NFL veterans, including Monte Coleman. The school was about to move to Division I-AA, an important step to Clinkscales because that meant he could still get a full scholarship, unlike if the school had stayed in Division II.

Much of the suspense about each of the players disappeared after Mustain chose Arkansas for the second time on January 16. However, the stress wasn't over for Beck Campbell or the parents of the other five who would sign on February 1.

Concerns were on their minds. Much like everything the team had done, the signing event — strictly ceremonial — since all the letters were inked well before the event, needed to be a once-in-a-lifetime thing, they said.

Although eager for signing day, Campbell was still recovering from putting together a 450-page commemorative book for the players and coaches. She had thought of the idea before the season and, after receiving permission from area newspapers, had taken time each day to download stories on the team. The money to bind the books had been donated by Tyson Foods and they were handed out at the season-ending banquet.

Despite her weariness both from the book and the recruitment of her son, Campbell worked with several parents to put together plans for the ceremony. Those plans included setting up a stage in the fieldhouse large enough for all six players to sit with their parents and sign at the same time. In front of each player the flag of their future school was draped across the table, and helmets from each of the schools sat on the table.

Planners made sure that each of the players received equal attention. That was after Perry Webb, Bartley's dad, expressed concern that only future Razorbacks would be celebrated.

"It's going to be great," Campbell said the day before. "The boys are going to love it.

"Of course, at this point, I can't wait to get some sleep."

• • •

More than 500 had gathered for the event, including Springdale players from the past and present and a host of casual fans not affiliated with the school. The cameras had lined the area surrounding where family members and school officials sat, and several people had gathered on the balcony which jutted out from the coaches offices.

The signing ceremony was history and the local media had completed their interviews. Only a handful of people remained inside the fieldhouse.

One of those was Annette Scogin, who replaced Malzahn as athletic director of the Springdale School District. Less than a year earlier, she had left an administrative job in the Little Rock School District to become volleyball coach at Springdale High. As soon as she was hired, those who paid attention believed she was in line to succeed Malzahn, either when he left for a college job or when the district's two high schools made it necessary for a full-time athletic director.

Scogin had done little to dispel the rumors, and less than three weeks after Malzahn's departure, her appointment was announced.

In her short time at Springdale, Scogin had come to respect Malzahn's work ethic and had appreciated that he had allowed her to work with him on the daily routine in the department. Both knew her future role.

Malzahn was recruiting for the Razorbacks and Scogin was melancholy about his absence that day.

"I wish Gus was here to see this," she said. "He had been such a big part of this.

"Don't get me wrong; everything went great. It just seemed like something was missing without him here."

To her left, standing in front of the stage where Malzahn had sat, Mitch Mustain fumbled as he tried to put the tiny television microphone on his dark suit.

The ceremony in Springdale had been broadcast nationally and now one of the recruiting shows wanted a few minutes on the air with the poster boy of the class. Once the microphone was attached, Mitch looked down for a moment while waiting his turn to answer more questions.

The camera's light came on and he looked up . . .

Afterword

IT HAS BEEN MORE THAN 18 MONTHS SINCE GUS MALZAHN AND I FIRST TALKED ABOUT THE POSSIBILITY OF THIS BOOK.

The words have long since been written, the people involved have gone their separate ways, and the dust has finally settled from the greatest high school football team many will ever see.

Much has changed in Springdale since February 1, 2006 — the day six Bulldogs signed full-ride college scholarships. That day was the culmination of greatness for some, while it marked the dawn of a new journey for others.

Har-Ber High opened varsity play on August 31, led by former Springdale High assistant Chris Wood and a handful of former Bulldogs who transferred. The Wildcats stunned even themselves that night, coming from behind to win their first game, 22–21 over MacArthur High in Lawton, Oklahoma.

"Those are still Springdale boys," Wood said afterward. "They are just wearing another helmet."

Springdale High opened its season with a victory as well, though the three-point win was a far cry from the usual blowouts of the season before. The Bulldogs, led by another former Malzahn assistant, Kevin Johnson, extended their winning streak to 16 games before being soundly defeated in their third game. That contest took place in Ohio as part of a nine-game showcase featuring teams from as far away as California and Florida. It also took place with assistant coach Kerry Winberry — having been talked into one more season — still on the sidelines.

The pipeline of talent in Springdale didn't end with the graduation of the seniors from the 2005 team. Tight end Zack Pianalto committed to defending national champion Texas in March, while kicker Alex Tejada elected to join his former teammates at Arkansas in August. Others — including quarterback Jeremy Paxton, linebacker Jamie Jones and safeties Eric Jones and Brandon Keaton — were expected to play in college as well.

As for Gus Malzahn and Mitch Mustain, well, they are doing what they always have — winning. After watching from the sidelines for most of Arkansas' season-opening loss to Southern California — with chants of "We want Mitch," echoing from the home crowd — Mustain entered the game in the fourth quarter.

On national television, he promptly led the Razorbacks on a scoring drive, highlighted by a long pass to former Springdale teammate Damian Williams and capped by a short touchdown run by none other than the golden-armed quarterback himself. The drive resulted in the wildest cheers of the evening, and Mustain was named the starter the next day.

He then led the Razorbacks to seven straight wins — becoming the first freshman in Arkansas history to do so in his first seven starts — highlighted by a win over No. 2 Auburn.

Ben Cleveland also made an early mark at Arkansas — catching a late touchdown pass from Mustain against Alabama in the third of those wins. Andrew Norman (Arkansas), Bartley Webb (Notre Dame) and Matt Clinkscales (Central Arkansas) each began their preparation for college football during the summer and were likely to redshirt during their freshman seasons.

Malzahn also made an early mark as offensive coordinator for the Razorbacks, dispelling the notion that the "high school" coach couldn't cut it in big-time college football. His professionalism and leadership quickly earned him the respect of the players, though his exact impact on play calling and his relationship with Arkansas coach Houston Nutt continues to be a subject for debate daily on Internet message boards and radio call-in shows.

As for me, I'm ever thankful.

I still realize that the angst provided during the recruiting moments of this book is what many will talk about. My hope is that, as one of the player's parents said, they realize that "everyone ended up where they needed to be."

High school football is only beginning to take the national stage. Where it goes from here, I have no idea.

Where it went with the 2005 Springdale Bulldogs was a once-in-a-lifetime moment.

TEAM ROSTER

Name	Height	Weight	Class	Position
Nathan Avey	6' 2"	231	Sr.	DT
Nestor Bahana	5' 2"	139	Jr.	CB
Bret Baker	5' 8"	135	Jr.	SE/CB
Dewayne Barnes	5' 9"	238	Jr.	OG
Juan Bautista	5' 7"	190	Jr.	OG
Matt Boyd	5' 11"	305	Sr.	DT
Michael Bush	5' 10"	196	Jr.	TB/LB
Ever Castillo	5' 8"	191	Jr.	OG
Jared Clark	6' 0"	245	Jr.	OT/DT
Ben Cleveland	6' 4"	231	Sr.	SE/LB
Jason Clinkscales	6' 1"	211	Sr.	OT/DT
Matt Clinkscales	6' 2"	206	Sr.	TB/LB
Hunter Collyar	5' 6"	138	Sr.	SE/C
Glenn Christopherson	5' 11"	122	Jr.	SE/C
Trey Crockett	5' 9"	146	Sr.	SE
Derek Crutchfield	6' 1"	177	Jr.	OT/DT
Chase Davis	5' 10"	186	Sr.	LB
Adam Delancy	5' 10"	205	Jr.	OG
Jake Duron	6' 4"	300	Jr.	DT
Grayson Edwards	6' 1"	180	Jr.	OT/DT
Andrew Fairchild	6' 0"	180	Jr.	LB
Aaron Finch	6' 2"	242	Sr.	DE
Kevin Flores	6' 0"	217	Sr.	OG
Josh Fohner	5' 9"	150	Soph.	QB/WR
Edwin Garcia	5' 10"	141	Jr.	CB
Jeremy Garcia	5' 10"	201	Sr.	DE
Russ Greenlee	5' 10"	182	Sr.	QB/CB
Justin Hathorn	5' 10"	140	Jr.	CB
Ryan Hoover	6' 2"	198	Sr.	LB
Brandon Ingram	5' 11"	186	Sr.	CB
Jeremy Jay	5' 10"	188	Jr.	LB
Brandon Johnson	6' 1"	167	Jr.	SE/S

Name	Height	Weight	Class	Position
Adam Jones	5' 8"	170	Sr.	TB
Eric Jones	5' 11"	173	Jr.	S
Jamie Jones	6' 0"	205	Jr.	TB/LB
Montana Jones	5' 9"	173	Jr.	OG/LB
Marek Kawasniak	5' 7"	179	Jr.	OG/DT
Neal Kuburich	6' 1"	217	Jr.	OG
Adam Larue	5' 10"	170	Jr.	FB
Colby Ledding	6' 1"	151	Jr.	FL
Lance Little	5' 8"	151	Jr.	CB
Steven Lloyd	5' 10"	153	Jr.	CB
Derek Marveggio	5' 10"	170	Sr.	LB
Cody Matthews	5' 8"	268	Jr.	C
Cory Meadors	5' 9"	155	Jr.	SE
Charlie McCormick	5' 9"	245	Jr.	OT
Ryan Moshtagh	5' 8"	190	Jr.	FB
Mitch Mustain	6' 3"	202	Sr.	QB
Andrew Norman	6' 2"	180	Sr.	SE/S
Matt Parson	5' 11"	221	Jr.	DE
Jared Pate	6' 0"	183	Jr.	OT/DT
Jeremy Paxton	6' 0"	179	Jr.	QB
James Penner	6' 3"	171	Jr.	DE
Chris Perkins	6' 2"	186	Sr.	S
Austin Pianalto	6' 1"	223	Sr.	OT
Drew Pianalto	6' 0"	170	Sr.	S
Justin Pianalto	6' 0"	155	Jr.	OG
Zack Pianalto	6' 4"	206	Jr.	FL/LB
Victor Pongonis	5' 9"	180	Sr.	FB
Mason Price	5' 10"	221	Sr.	C
Clint Pruitt	5' 7"	168	Jr.	CB
Allen Reed	6' 0"	297	Sr.	OG/DT
Brooks Reimer	6' 2"	180	Soph.	DE
Jason Ross	6' 0"	193	Sr.	DE

Name	Height	Weight	Class	Position
Chase Sanders	5' 11"	205	Sr.	LB
Terry Sanders	5' 5"	142	Jr.	TB
Chris Simco	5' 10"	155	Jr.	LB
Luke Stamp	6' 0"	245	Jr.	OT/DT
Cory Stewart	5' 10"	187	Sr.	LB
Eric Stewart	5' 9"	187	Sr.	FB/LB
Nick Taylor	6' 0"	246	Sr.	C
Alex Tejada	5' 10"	170	Jr.	K
Chris Thompson	6' 1"	183	Sr.	LB
Jordan Thompson	5' 11"	185	Sr.	LB
Thomas Tiner	6' 0"	168	Jr.	LB
Michael Upton	5' 8"	135	Soph.	CB
Garrott VanBebber	6' 0"	165	Sr.	S
Bartley Webb	6' 7"	291	Sr.	OT
Matt White	5' 11"	223	Jr.	OT/DT
Damian Williams	6' 1"	185	Sr.	TB/S
Brandon Windham	5' 10"	275	Sr.	DT
Justin Wood	6' 2"	231	Sr.	OG
Josh Wright	6' 0"	192	Jr.	DE